Sun Yat-sen

Americans wonder more and more how China came to be Communist and why this traditionally friendly country is now so hostile to us.

The search leads back to the Chinese Revolution of 1911. We need to know how that revolution began, who began it, and why. And the key figure in the story of the revolution —and of the direction taken since the revolution—is Sun Yat-sen.

As a boy and as a young man, Sun aimed at awakening his country, freeing her from Manchu or foreign rulers, modernizing her, and giving her a place among the world's leading nations. He traveled widely, appealing to Chinese students around the world. They flocked to him, and he became the voice of stirring China.

Cornelia Spencer tells Sun Yat-sen's life story with the authority and understanding gained from her own extensive background in China.

Sun Yat-sen, founder of the Chinese Republic.

Sun Yat-sen

FOUNDER OF THE CHINESE REPUBLIC

Cornelia Spencer

Illustrated

The John Day Company · New York

Books by Cornelia Spencer

THREE SISTERS

CHINA TRADER

ELIZABETH: ENGLAND'S MODERN QUEEN

THE EXILE'S DAUGHTER

THE LAND OF THE CHINESE PEOPLE

MADE IN CHINA

MADE IN INDIA

MADE IN JAPAN

THE MISSIONARY

NEHRU OF INDIA

STRAIGHT FURROW

UNDERSTANDING THE JAPANESE

SEVEN THOUSAND ISLANDS

ROMULO: VOICE OF FREEDOM

ANCIENT CHINA

THE SONG IN THE STREETS

MORE HANDS FOR MAN

CLAIM TO FREEDOM

HOW ART AND MUSIC SPEAK TO US

PEARL S. BUCK: REVEALING THE HUMAN HEART

KEEPING AHEAD OF MACHINES

SUN YAT-SEN

Author's Note

While some incidents and conversations reported in this book have been put into direct form for dramatic effect, all are authentic and no fictional events have been created. Direct quotations are indicated by numbers in the text which relate to references listed at the end of the book.

CONTENTS

Sun Yat-sen

A TASTE FOR FREEDOM

1. Lured by the World Beyond

A British ship, the *Grannoch,* was loading Chinese emigrants at Macao on the South China coast, on a day in 1879. She was booked for Hawaii and she was filling rapidly. The California Gold Rush had started a flow of Chinese laborers to the western hemisphere a generation before this time, and that flow had never stopped.

The ship's English sailors seemed not to see the milling, pushing people with their countless cloth-tied bundles or pigskin boxes who surged around them, or to hear the din of shouts and curses dramatized by wavings and beckonings. They paid no attention to young lads who excitedly darted in and out of the crowd. Even if they had they would not have been likely to single out a sun-bronzed country boy whose name was Sun Yat-sen. Only one thing might have made them look at him a second time. This was the expression of delighted, curious anticipation in his unusually large eyes. Although none of his family had walked the thirty or so miles from his home village to see him off, he gave no sign of having run away.

Sun Yat-sen was twelve. He was on his way to Hawaii where his much older brother, Sun Mei, had gone in 1871, and was now doing a big business in raising sugarcane. It seemed to the boy that it had taken an endlessly long time to reach this moment. Everything had pulled him toward it, but one great obstacle had always postponed it—his age. He was too young, his father said, too young for everything except memorizing the Chinese classics in the village school and helping his father with his farm work. But he had not been too young for his dreams. These dreams he had had as far back as he could remember, daydreams of the world beyond the Hsiang Shan or Fragrant Hills that surrounded his home village, Choyhung, and gave their name to the district and its chief town.

The dreams could not be stopped for the outer world reached in and touched the little farming village because of its location. A bay of the ocean lay just over the hills and small seacraft came there. Seamen often told listening boys stories about other people and places, or recounted bloody pirate tales. Macao, a port built by Portuguese traders in the sixteenth century, was the oldest foreign port of all China. Canton, up the West River, had become a treaty port two dozen years before Sun Yat-sen was born, and clipper ships from many faraway places sailed to Whampoa, a point twelve miles below Canton, which was as far as they could navigate. Hong Kong was the deep-water port, and when the British took possession of it after the Opium War treaties, trading ships from around the world began to gather in its harbor. Hong Kong was only about eighty miles from Canton and half as far as that from Macao.

Choyhung, then, for all its being tucked away among the Kwangtung Province hills, was skirted by river and ocean, close to ports that had become international.

The outside had reached into Sun Yat-sen's boyhood not only because of the place where he lived. It had affected him more intimately through his own family. His father was a farmer and his mother was a country woman with old-fashioned bound feet, but two uncles, brothers of his father, had gone to California during the Gold Rush. Steamship agents had combed the villages all around telling how quickly one could get rich picking up gold nuggets on the shining shores, but not mentioning the fact that they were looking for cheap labor. By 1851, 25,000 Chinese were working in California, some as placer miners, but more as laborers and cooks. Sun Yat-sen's two uncles had gone, leaving their families behind in the Sun household. After years had passed the aunts learned that one of their husbands had been lost at sea while the other had died in California.

When Yat-sen was only a little boy of six or so, Sun Mei, his brother, who was fifteen years older than he, had emigrated to Hawaii to work in developing some low-lying land not far from Pearl Harbor. The Chinese called the Hawaiian Islands the Sandalwood Islands because they imported a great deal of this sweet-smelling wood from there. Sun Mei's first letter home had not arrived until a year after he had left. It had been a never-to-be-forgotten family event. No one in the family could read, though Yat-sen was learning to in the village school. They had had to take the letter to the village scribe, who read it aloud while they, and others who crowded around curiously, listened in. But it had been hard to understand the words even when one

heard them so the scribe had explained them at great
length. When he had given a short lecture on each phrase,
the family at least had known that Sun Mei was well and
prospering.

Before long Yat-sen had learned to read such a letter
aloud himself while the family sat around the dining table
listening proudly. At last they could picture yellow beaches
and soil that grew fine crops of grapes, oranges, pineapples
and strange trees—and best of all, a place where one could
make a good living.

So Hawaii had reached in and touched not only Choyhung, but the Sun household in personal ways. Yet the hills
had still seemed like a high wall to Yat-sen the boy, a wall
he had had to scale somehow in order to be free. The local
tea shop, like a corner drugstore, had helped. Men gathered
there to sip tea and discuss the news and exchange gossip.
The tea shop had been like a small window through the
thick wall. Yat-sen had often hung about there trying to get
fresh glimpses of the outside world.

In 1877 Sun Mei had made a visit home. The family
had given a great feast to celebrate his coming. Yat-sen had
been ten years old by then and he had had a wonderful
time. He had hung on every word his brother had said. If
only *he* could go to Hawaii, too. His dreams had focused on
this one hope.

"Two years ago the Hawaiian government made a treaty
with America," Sun Mei had explained to his parents one
day, "not to charge any duty or import tax on her sugar.
This gives us a good market for our sugar because the
United States is a big country. And now," he had gone on,
"Pearl Harbor is being made into a great naval station.
American ships take on coal there—such ships!" he had

finished, drawing a deep breath. His little brother's eyes had been shining.

"You talk about that place as if you no longer belonged in Choyhung or were the oldest son of the Sun family," the mother had said sadly.

"No, that is not so," Sun Mei had answered quickly. "I was only describing what is happening there." He had stopped and reached into his pocket and brought out a handful of coins and poured them on the table. "These are for you, and there will be more. I will provide enough for a better house," he had added, watching their astonished faces. Then before they had begun to breath normally again he had said, "I have come, too, to ask you to find me a wife, to take back with me." His face had flushed red beneath its bronze. His mother's expression had first been joyful and then the happiness had faded. So, the daughter-in-law, too, would have to go to that strange place, and she would never see the grandchildren.

Sun Yat-sen's eyes had fastened on his brother, unconscious of his parents. When would Sun Mei be going back, he had wondered. He would have to pay passage for himself and his wife, and then there were the wedding expenses to be met. How could he manage it all—but there was that heap of coins. His father had counted them carefully, his face puzzled. Of course, the boy had thought, Sun Mei would have plenty of money for the wedding, for the passages for himself and his wife, for everything. Yat-sen wanted to go to Hawaii. Would his brother take him? Dared he put his question into words? His mouth had gone dry. No words had come.

At this moment, Yat-sen would never forget, Sun Mei had looked around at them all. "I have a plan," he had

announced. The flush had left his face for now he had become all businessman, thinking and calculating as he
talked. "The Hawaiian government will give a bonus for
each emigrant to the islands who signs a five-year work
contract. I have a friend from near Canton who will help
me find emigrants to fill a ship. The bonus money will be
our commission, for the people who go will gladly consider
it their payment to us for transporting them." He had been
gazing at his fingers and measuring them against each other
while he talked. Then he had looked at his father and
around the circle at each one in turn. His father's expression had been openly pleased and proud. "A good head, a
good head," he had commented. "Who else would have
thought up such a scheme!"

Sun Mei's eyes had stopped on his little brother. "Yat-sen
is plenty big to go back with me," he had said thoughtfully.
"He looks strong and fit." The boy's heart had begun to
thump against his ribs and he had turned appealingly to his
parents. He had not needed words of his own for Sun Mei
had spoken for him. But of course he had known his mother
would object, mothers always. . . . Instead it had been his
father. "No," he had said firmly, "he is too young to go.
Besides, we cannot have both sons away from the household."

"Two uncles and one son away are already too much to
bear," his mother had put in quickly. "My sons' father is
right. Yat-sen must stay here."

"He would be with me. I would look after him," Sun Mei
had continued. "There are good schools there, modern
schools—"

"Modern!" his father had interrupted. "Such schools do

not teach the classics, and they have strange religions. They are no place for any son of mine."

The older brother had given the younger a quick sympathetic look. It had been clear to both of them that their parents were not going to agree to Yat-sen's going. Perhaps there might be some way when he was older. His eyes had dropped to his hands, clasped tightly together in his lap. He had been bitterly disappointed but he was not going to let anyone see the tears that had rushed to his eyes.

After Sun Mei had gone back to Hawaii he and his friend in Canton had worked on their plan to engage an emigrant ship. Almost two years had passed before this could be done. Then they had the *Grannoch,* British, and weighing 2,000 tons. She would take twenty days to reach Honolulu.

When Sun Mei had again at this time asked his parents about Yat-sen's going, they had agreed at once. Perhaps his being two years older had made the difference; perhaps the fact that they had seen that Sun Mei was well established in his business and with a home of his own. When the day for sailing had arrived, Yat-sen had made his way to Macao, alone.

He could scarcely wait to experience his new freedom, yet when the hubbub of loading was over, the cables were released and the crowded ship started to move slowly away from shore, the boy had strange, mixed feelings. He was so proud to be Chinese, so proud of the history and culture of his people, but he was ashamed of their unwillingness to modernize. He had been told that his South China was more open-minded than any other part of the country, and yet how ignorant and old-fashioned people were, even there. How willing they were to stay under the rule of the "foreign" Manchus of the Ch'ing Dynasty in Peking!

In his own village things were still going on just as they had for centuries. Old-fashioned binding of the feet of little girls, old-fashioned worship of the gods in the village temple, old-fashioned festivals in their honor, old-fashioned schooling that was only memorizing book after book of classics without understanding a word of what they really said, continued. It made him blush to think of such things. And yet their province, Kwangtung, was truly a gateway to the world. Ships sailed in and out; strange people came and went just a few miles from his home. Why was it that no one in his village except Sun Mei, and long ago his uncles, wanted to learn anything new, or change things? Even Sun Mei was not really interested in Choyhung, only in a new house for his parents. He never said anything about the Manchus in Peking or about modernizing China.

Why did *he* have to worry about his country as he stood gazing into the sea, watching it change from river-yellow to sea-blue as the ship reached the open ocean? He was going to be with Sun Mei in Honolulu! He pushed all other thoughts away impatiently and turned to look at the people around him, especially the strange British sailors.

He wanted to explore the ship. He climbed down a precarious winding ladder to the engine room, crowded with machinery, where cylinders belched steam. The stokers kept steadily at their work. Their faces were livid with their effort and with the heat which came from the glowing coals. They were so dirty he could scarcely tell their nationality. In a moment a sailor was after him, chattering something and motioning him back to the deck.

As the days passed he watched the Westerners. He thought they did everything well. He was impressed by their efficiency. And then a strange thing happened. One of the

British sailors died. Instead of putting his body in a sealed coffin to take it to his home when they could, they buried him at sea. Yat-sen, of course, could not understand English and he had no idea what was about to happen when the burial began. He saw something sewed up in canvas. He watched as the Union Jack was spread over it. He heard the ship's bell toll while the crew and officers gathered around what he knew now must be the body. The captain read something quickly from a small book. A bugle blew. The body was weighted with iron and dropped splashing over into the sea. How terribly cold and harsh, Yat-sen thought. None of the poor fellow's family had been there. There had been no proper ceremonies, no waiting for an auspicious day. Worst of all, the sailor would have no grave! The boy turned away to walk along the crowded deck, shaken and confused by the incident.

But beneath his feet the steel ship was steadily throbbing under the regular propulsion of her engines. She was pushing her way across hundreds of miles of unfathomed ocean. The same red-faced Britishers who could drop a dead man over the side to the monsters of the sea knew how to build ships and navigate them, how to force the nations of the world to trade with them even when they did not want to. One day Yat-sen climbed to the bridge out of curiosity and in the instant before he was ordered down, glimpsed dials, steering wheel and all kinds of handles and magical things. The ship became more of a mystery rather than less as the time passed.

"My people have to learn," he thought again and again while the twenty days went by. "They have to learn how to make machinery and ships and trains." Even more, he knew already, they had to stop looking back to the past and begin

to look ahead to the future. The real trouble was having
those Manchus on the throne in Peking. He was sure of
that. During the long hours when he had nothing to do but
gaze at the sea, he began to imagine what it would be like if
his people rose up and overthrew their government. He
knew from school that it had happened many times in
China's history when rulers oppressed the people too much.
Perhaps a time was coming when the Manchus would have
to be gotten rid of. Yat-sen's eyes turned from their deep
brown to almost black when he thought of this tremendous
idea. He glanced quickly around. Could anyone see his
thoughts? No one had noticed him, nor would anyone possibly have been interested in what the emigrant boy on his
way to Hawaii was thinking while he studied the sea.

2. Initiation to the West in Hawaii

When the Hawaiian Islands first came into sight, Sun Yat-sen could scarcely believe they were real. The sandy beaches fringed by palm groves set against a background of cloud-covered mountains still seemed only something he had so often dreamed about. As the ship neared King's Pier in Honolulu, he felt an easy-going leisure among the waiting people instead of the bustling energy of the South China harbor workers he was used to. Horse-drawn vehicles moved along the main street toward what Yat-sen later learned were the municipal buildings. Large warehouses rose on all sides of the pier itself. Beyond he glimpsed shacks and vegetable gardens. Great spaces simply lay open and unused. This seemed most strange because where he came from every inch of land was worked for something.

All this was only a quick first impression which he got while the ship was docking. Then suddenly Sun Mei was leaping up the narrow gangway and soon stood beside him. It was only two years or so since they had seen each other in Choyhung, and yet in that time Yat-sen had grown and changed. The three weeks at sea when he was without family had taught him a certain self-confidence. He was shy but he was not afraid. He had thought of Choyhung and his parents many times and had sometimes even been a little homesick. Now all that was over and he was only glad to be here in Hawaii.

"I have written a letter to our parents. How can I find a way to send it to them?" he asked his brother. Of course they would not be able to read it but they could take it to the village scribe. Yat-sen could just hear the scribe's sing-song voice that would all but destroy the meaning of what he had said. All that already seemed so far away and hard to believe that he almost smiled.

"The post office is down the street, on the right," Sun Mei said pointing as they pushed through the bewildered crowd of emigrants and past heaps of baggage. Post office? Yat-sen made out a red brick building with a tower and clock. They went directly there and paid the cost of sending the letter. The incident stayed in his mind for many years and he later told an American friend, "The old Honolulu post office still stands out in my mind very clearly. I looked upon it as a wonder-house, for they told me that by merely stamping and addressing a letter and dropping it in a box, I could send it back to China as speedily as a ship could go, without having to wait for weeks or even months to find some emigrant to act as a personal messenger."[1]

He was astonished at how orderly everything was. Most of all he was surprised at the way the native people had accepted the leadership of the Americans. There seemed to be no fights or arguments. He did not see any law courts or *yamen,* which were to be found in every Chinese town of any size and plagued his country. At home everyone dreaded being taken to the *yamen* because they had learned to expect injustice rather than justice there. There must be real law and order here and that was why the people did not resent the Americans, he decided. He watched everything eagerly, studied what he saw and asked Sun Mei endless questions.

"These people must like the Americans," he told his brother as they spent his first day walking around the town.

"Why not?" his brother answered. "They're improving everything, building big businesses and giving us farmers and fruit-growers good profits. They are fine managers and know how to do things."

What Sun Mei said was true, but it did not quite answer Yat-sen's questions. There was still something more to it, something it was hard for him to put into words. The atmosphere was free. No one seemed to bother anyone else. He did see one policeman arresting a man, but the man did not cower in terror; no great crowd gathered around as they would have in Choyhung, waiting for an incident. No one said, "He'll be taken to the *yamen,*" as if it were practically the same as being given a death sentence. No, that kind of fear of being treated unjustly did not appear to be here at all. It was this feeling of freedom, of nothing hanging over even in a place held by a foreign power that made him love Hawaii almost at once. All that day in Honolulu he kept thinking about it. The Hawaiian people did not seem to be subject to the Americans. That was the word—subject. Hawaii did not seem like a colonial possession. It was not

like Macao or Canton or Hong Kong, at least not from
what he had heard, for he had not been to all three of
them.

Yat-sen was almost shocked to see that everything here
was ordinary to Sun Mei for he had grown so used to it that
he no longer was aware of it. His mind was strictly on his
business. Sometimes he did not seem to hear his younger
brother's surprised statements, or even bother to answer his
questions. After a few days they set out for Sun Mei's place
at Ewa in the Pearl Harbor area, not far from the city of
Honolulu. Yat-sen really had less idea than ever what to
expect. He knew that his brother was a rice farmer now,
and he had heard him mention a store, too, but that was
almost all. Rice-growing was very familiar, for the province
of Kwangtung where the Sun family lived was a rice-growing area, but they had never been storekeepers.

When the two brothers' father was a young man he had
once left the farm to go to Macao to learn tailoring, but he
had soon drawn back from it because it was too strange.
Instead, he married a girl at home and settled into rice-
growing. Yat-sen had helped in the fields as far back as he
could remember. He had often run to the village stores for
his mother and had studied the interesting things he found
there, but it had never occurred to him that he might one
day take part in storekeeping.

When they reached Ewa, which was nothing more than a
small village, Sun Mei at once set his brother to work in the
store that he carried on in addition to his farming. What a
pusher Sun Mei was, the boy thought, doing two things at
once. No wonder he had been making so much money that
he could pour a heap of coins on the dining table at home

that time and dazzle them all. And the coins had been nothing compared to other money he had later sent home.

Sun Mei patiently taught him how to keep the accounts written in Chinese and made him practice the abacus every day. Yat-sen's schooling was used hard. But the village people who came to buy things could not speak Chinese and Yat-sen had to learn to understand their dialect. He gradually began to speak it for it was much easier than Chinese, which had many tone variations. Sun Mei knew how to speak English and that was what Yat-sen really wanted to learn, but for the time being there seemed to be little chance that Sun Mei would take time to teach him. He was far too busy.

The boy settled in to being a clerk while his brother went off to the rice fields two miles away or into the city on business. Sometimes when there were no customers, Yat-sen wondered if it were still all a dream. Here he sat in a small dark store surrounded by rice sacks, brooms and brushes, sweet cakes and candies and imported medicines, trying to keep books and straining to understand the foreign language of a strange, gay, new kind of people. Through the open door he glimpsed marshlands, sugarcane fields and rice paddies broken here and there by clumps of tapioca or cassava bushes. It was all strange and different, but in this new place, with the ocean right out there, with great ships coming and going from west to east and east to west, he was again chained to a village, bound to a store and responsible to his family in his brother.

When the first few weeks of learning his job and becoming accustomed to the people had passed, Yat-sen found his life deadly dull. Although he fought back the feeling, he was bitterly disappointed. What did Sun Mei have in mind for him? Was he just going to use him in this store? Was that all he wanted him for? It was hard to believe that, although it was traditional for sons of a family to help each other. There was nothing to do but wait and do his work as well as he possibly could.

Yat-sen soon found that Sun Mei had made a reputation for himself as a successful rice farmer and businessman. He was thought of as rather well off. He was ambitious, too, but he had a strong feeling of family responsibility. Yat-sen could not guess that Sun Mei had been thinking ahead, shrewdly, and had plans for him. He would give his little brother a practical taste of business, and, if he showed ability, he would build him into the business as his partner. This partnership could take the place of wages now and would in the end make Yat-sen secure for the future. If this plan seemed justified, Sun Mei would give Yat-sen a Western education so that he would have the English language and be able to move up in the business world. There were good Western schools in Honolulu and they were one reason why Sun Mei had been so anxious for the boy to come with him that first time. Now he saw that Yat-sen was bright and that he could be a great asset in his business when he had an education. At the same time his future would be taken care of by the partnership arrangement.

Sun Mei had kept his eyes and ears alert to school possibilities. He had found out only good things about a certain school opened by a Bishop Willis of the Anglican Church. The bishop lived on the school grounds and this meant that he could supervise it closely. Iolani, as it was generally known, stood just outside Honolulu, on grounds stretching along a white beach and facing the ocean. Although the official name of Iolani was Bishop's College School, it was really a secondary school for Hawaiian boys. The fee was $100 a year, which was a very large sum in the nineteenth century, but Sun Mei did not hold back because of it. Instead, he made arrangements for his brother to enroll in the fall of 1879 just a few months after he arrived in the islands. The question of Yat-sen's birthplace must have been overlooked when Sun Mei filed an application for his brother, because Sun Mei was well known as an immigrant from China rather than a Hawaiian.

Yat-sen was excited and jubilant when Sun Mei told him about his plans for him. Now the chain that had been binding him had broken. He was free and stepping out into a new world. But when he went to school on the opening day he was soon overwhelmed by a babel of strange, impossible language. It was English and he found to his horror that all the classes were conducted in it, and he had picked up only a half dozen phrases by this time. All but one of the teachers were British and that one was the English instructor! The school seemed to take it for granted that the students came from Western backgrounds. History stressed the chronology of the kings and queens of England, assumed that all the boys knew something about Jewish and Christian civilization, and taught only European forms of music. For the first few days the Chinese boy in his long blue cotton gown with his shining braid of hair, or queue, simply sat and listened as the queer English sounds flowed around him. He did what others showed him he was supposed to do until he gradually learned the phrases that were orders or directions.

When two weeks had passed Sun Yat-sen could stammer a little English, and then suddenly he discovered the language had a system to it and he began to speak it. Once he

had the alphabet and some idea of phonetics, he had rules
to follow. The beautiful English diction which he was to use
the rest of his life began here. He found written English
much easier than spoken after the hieroglyphics of Chinese,
which had to be memorized. The wonderful alphabet
seemed a key to everything.

But not everything was as easy as language turned out to
be. His long shiny queue was a real problem because the
boys simply could not resist torturing him by pulling it. At
first the older boys were the worst ones, and then when they
grew ashamed of doing it, they instigated the younger ones
to do it for them. Sun Yat-sen was muscular and strong and
he turned on them and punished them hard.

One day some of the boys who really admired him for his
courage said, "Why don't you just cut off your pigtail?" He
had thought of doing that but he had decided that his queue
was more than a personal hairstyle. It was a symbol of China
under the Manchus. They had imposed the queue on the
Chinese as a brand or mark of their servitude. This symbol
could be taken away properly only when China was free. If
some cut their hair and others did not it would break up
the solidarity of his people, Yat-sen thought. They must
endure their slavery until they could throw it off as a people. He talked this idea over with some of the Chinese
students and they agreed with him even though being
Hawaiian-born, they had never worn their hair in queues.
The teasing gradually became uninteresting and the question of Sun Yat-sen's pigtail was forgotten. The problems of
the English language and teasing had been mastered.

Yat-sen had other experiences that were almost pure delight. He had never learned to swim, but now he did for the
schoolboys swam in a large clear pool. The school held fire

drills and had its own fire brigade. He took part enthusiastically. Back at home when there had been a fire in
Choyhung, nothing had been done because nothing could
be done. There was no water supply and no plan to provide
any. He saw now how much could be accomplished by
organizing people to work together, even schoolboys. He
had never heard Western music before and he was astonished at its mathematical system and its reasonableness. He
began to test his own voice in the religious music of the
Anglican services and felt a glow of satisfaction when he
was one of those who were chosen for the choir. When he
was gowned in a surplice and took part in the processionals
from the school to St. Andrews Church in the city he felt it
was highly important. The religious rituals and routines
seemed full of mystery and beauty to him. Since Iolani was
a church school, all the boys were taught religious history
and Christian theology. Yat-sen took the instruction seriously and asked no questions. Look at how strong the Western nations, the Christian nations, were! Look at their scientific progress and their skill! Theirs was not a religion of
foolish idols and superstitious practices like those of the
people in Choyhung, but a religion based on a high regard
for God, whom Confucius, too, had revered as Heaven, and
of brotherly love, which both Confucius and Gautama
Buddha had asked their followers to show, before all they
had taught had been buried under stupid forms.

Sun Yat-sen could not have fought off Christianity's at-
traction for him even if he had tried. He had good men as
teachers, men who tried to put what they taught into practice. The boy was at an age when the symbolism of the
religion appealed to him. He liked the idea of the sacra-
ments taken to remember the last supper of Jesus and his

disciples; he was moved at the theory of the Trinity including the Spirit sent out to live among men. Most of all he was impressed by the sincerity of his instructors. One day he innocently tried to explain his feelings to Sun Mei and said he thought of joining the Anglican Church. He was so intent on what he was saying that he did not notice the expression of shock and horror on his non-Christian brother's face. Sun Mei did not say anything at the time but he made a mental note to check Yat-sen's interest in Christianity.

During his third year at the school, military drills were started. Sun Yat-sen took part in them and did exceptionally well. But his work in English literature was his chief interest and everything else was secondary to that. As the year moved toward its end, he heard whispers that he was to receive a prize on graduation day.

Commencement exercises were held in the summer of 1882. King Kalakaua presented the prizes while the Queen and the Princess looked on. It was a great occasion. When Sun Yat-sen's name was called, he walked across the stage which was set in the open in view of the sea, looking tall for his age and almost too brown to be Chinese. He still wore his hair in a queue but he was dressed in shorts and a jacket instead of Chinese clothes. He received the second prize in English grammar. The prize was two books, one the story of a missionary in China, the other a leather-bound Bible.

Three years had gone by since he reached Hawaii and now Sun Mei said that he must return to China to see the parents, and that he must have them find him a wife. Sun Mei's real reason for hurrying the boy home without further education in Hawaii was that he felt strongly that Yat-sen must be taken away from Christian influences. It was a good thing to learn techniques and know-how from the

West, but Christianity was dangerous. What if Yat-sen were to abandon his responsibility to his ancestors and family! He had not brought his brother to this place to make a revolutionary Christian out of him!

Sun Yat-sen was very much disappointed at the thought of going home, for he had been dreaming of going much further in his education. He had worked hard and done well. But of course he could not argue with his older brother, who had paid his bills and done so much to help him. For the rest of the summer he simply worked quietly in the store just as he had before he entered school and during each holiday. After all, he consoled himself, he and his brother were partners in the business in Hawaii.

3. Young Man in Rebellion

When the eighteen-year-old Sun Yat-sen saw the Hawaiian Islands disappear over the horizon, he thought of his first glimpse of them. How much had happened to him in those few years! He knew that he had changed because of what he had seen and what he had experienced. Yet one strong idea had not been altered. It had only grown much clearer, had grown from a vague feeling to a strong conviction. It was that only a free people could make their own life and shape their own destiny. Why should the Chinese be so bound by their past, or allow foreign nations to control them? The Hawaiians had learned from the West instead of letting themselves be exploited. They were changing themselves as they wanted to change. The Chinese were going to have to free themselves, too, and move on into the modern world.

Looking out on the great Pacific Ocean as the days on the ship passed, the young man turned this idea over and over in his mind. How could the Chinese be made to change? No one had ever tried to make them do such a thing, unless it was that man Hung Hsiu-ch'üan who had led the Taiping Rebellion a half-century ago. Of course there had been many secret societies down through Chinese history that had tried to upset dynasties that were not to their liking. But they had been formed because people could no longer stand the hardships they lived under, not because of any dream of a new kind of China. Such rebellions had been a throwing off rather than a rebuilding.

Sun Yat-sen had heard his own village people talk about Hung sometimes. The Taiping, or Great Peace, Rebellion had begun right in Canton and had swept through the Yangtze River Valley for fourteen years, ending just two years before Sun Yat-sen himself was born. Hung and his men had even taken Nanking and held it for more than ten years with the help of a secret society called the Triads. Yat-sen thought a lot about the fact that Hung had dreamed of a new China because of Christianity. Hung had learned something about Christianity from a missionary pamphlet and decided that God was calling him to save his people. He used large parts of the Old Testament but rejected much of the New, to strengthen his position. Out of such ideas he had developed a rebellion that was successful for a time. Of course he had succeeded because of the suffering of the Chinese people. Famines, unjust taxation, wicked officials and foreign traders who cooperated with pirates and merchants in carrying on trade in opium had all taken part in bringing the situation to a crisis, and Hung had taken advantage of it. Missionaries had hoped that Hung would become a great religious leader and succeed where they had failed. But he was a political leader rather than a religious one, in the end, and tried to make such reforms as redistributing land, reducing taxes and equalizing the sexes in Chinese society.

Young Sun Yat-sen knew that people said Hung's leadership had not been strong enough to carry out his plans. His organization had been poor and not enough people had come forward to help him. Yet he had had something. He had at least seen that China had to change from the foundation up, and he had gotten this conviction from a Christian Western world.

The days aboard ship were soon gone and ragged South China hills, seagoing junks, and fishing boats made up the landscape again. At last the ship entered the mountain-encircled harbor of Hong Kong. Passengers going on to Canton as Yat-sen was, had to transfer to smaller craft here. Sun and some others boarded a sand junk bound for that city, but they had to first go through customs at a small island in the Hong Kong harbor. Their captain warned them to prepare "gifts" or tips for the customs officers to make things easier all around.

The Manchu officers, dressed in their black gowns, wearing silver swords and belts and blue-buttoned caps, searched the baggage. They demanded payments. All the passengers including Sun submitted to what were in many cases unjust charges, just to avoid trouble. Now, Sun thought to himself, the whole business was over with, anyhow, but he had barely finished strapping his baggage up again when a second group of officers leaped aboard saying that they were to collect *likin*. *Likin* was a trade tax begun at the time of the Taiping Rebellion to help meet the cost of bringing it to an end. Sun submitted to the examination of his baggage once more, but when a third group of officials appeared, rattling their swords and saying that they were looking for opium smugglers, he was really angry. There was nothing to do but unstrap everything another time and give another tip. By this time he was boiling mad and when a fourth group of officers came aboard saying they were looking for petroleum smugglers, he refused to touch a strap. The captain of the sand junk begged him to comply for the sake of all the others who were meekly doing what they were told. Sun refused. He began to lecture the other passengers for submitting to such demands. He offered to help the captain get justice when they reached Canton. He said he would even appeal to a higher court. The captain laughed loudly.

"Justice? Do you think there is any justice to be gotten?" he shouted. "You are only a young fool who does not know the world, getting us all into trouble. You and your foreign ideas." He glared at Sun and Sun knew his own face was red with anger, something that every well-brought-up Chinese tried to avoid. Even worse, because of him the ship could not move on. It was held there the rest of that day, through the night and on into the next day. Sun tried to explain why he had refused to open his baggage a fourth time, discussed the principle of justice that was involved and insisted that people could not submit or there would never be a change for the better; but the weary, angry passengers were not interested in what he, a swaggering young upstart, thought. At last in desperation the captain paid what was called a fine but was really a bribe, and the ship sailed on to the Canton anchorage. When Sun stepped ashore he was still talking about corrupt officials. "Aren't you going to do anything about this? Are you just going to keep on submitting?" he asked the people around him.[1] They only hurried on.

When at last Sun reached Choyhung, his home people welcomed him royally. They feasted him and asked many questions about Hawaii, but the questions disappointed him. No one was interested in how the islands were governed, or asked about their law courts, schools or transportation. They asked only about the kinds of food, and how rich people were and other superficial things. He was still so annoyed by the incident of the customs officers that before he knew it he found himself lecturing his home-town people about the wicked government officials partly because they showed little interest in the outside world, and that angered him again.

"You go along with statements about the generosity and grace of the emperor, and praise him for his government. You say that the government is good but the officials are bad. What is the difference between government and officials, I ask you?" he demanded. "When the officials are corrupt, the government is corrupt, too."[2] Even though the villagers had to admit that these words had a familiar ring to them, for surely Confucius had said something like that, they were horrified when Yat-sen talked like this. His parents, too, thought he had come back with some very strange ideas, and worst of all he was scolding them although they had spent so much to welcome him home. Friends of the family discussed him privately and pitied his parents. They should never have let him go away. Too bad that he was so unlike his older brother, who had given his parents money for their fine new home.

Sun Yat-sen spoke out more and more. He became a young reformer who addressed any crowd that would listen to him, for he was reading newspapers and periodicals and forming his own political ideas. He denounced the local

court, or *yamen*, as well as the national government, pointing out that the Chinese paid heavier taxes to the Manchu
government than any people should and had absolutely
nothing to show for them. Roads were not improved,
bridges were not repaired, transportation was miserable. He
suggested simple things like coordinating the days when
country fairs were held with village market days so that
more could be sold to larger crowds and better profits
would be realized.

"We'll have to get rid of the Manchus," he said more and
more often. "They're foreigners. Whether you know it or
not we are ruled by foreigners!" What was the use of talking? he thought desperately. Not even his own village people knew enough to realize that the Manchus were foreign.
They were so used to corrupt government that they never
even questioned the justice of a practice or a law. They only
hoped to stay out of the clutches of officials, to never be
dragged to the *yamen*. He saw that they were terrified at
what he was saying. Soon he realized that they were afraid
to be seen in his company or listening to him.

Sun Yat-sen definitely connected progress with Christianity and thought of China's religions as backward-looking.
He had seen wonders in Hawaii, accomplished, he was sure,
because of Christianity's civilizing influence. He understood
some of Confucius' philosophical theories that he had
learned in his early schooling, and although they had
seemed far away at that time, he now began to see that they
could be useful. The only trouble was that no one was interested in applying them. The Christians he had come to
know had, he thought, at least tried to apply what they
believed, and he had seen some of the results at Iolani.

Father Sun was old now, for Yat-sen had not been born

until his middle age. The young man knew that he would
never be able to make him change or even understand. His
mother was old-fashioned, too. She had once started to bind
the feet of Sun Yat-sen's sister. He still remembered the
little girl's bitter crying and how relieved he had been when
the plan was given up. However upset and unhappy he was
now he knew that he had done the right thing by returning
to Choyhung, for as a dutiful son he must try to help his
father. But he soon found that he could not be a dutiful son
in any real sense. He rebelled against the ignorance of the
whole village. He could not blame them, but they were still
ignorant and he hated that ignorance. At first he was entirely alone in his rebellion against the past. Then he found
a friend, a sixteen-year-old boy named Lu Hao-tung, who
had come to town for the funeral of his father. The Lu
family had moved to Shanghai years before but the family
burial plot was still here. Lu had not only lived in Shanghai,
he spoke English and he was a church member. Sun and Lu
became friends and because they often talked about Christianity, although Sun had not joined the church, Sun called
Lu his "doctrinal friend."

Lu Hao-tung liked to talk about the Taiping Rebellion.
He had made a kind of specialty of the subject and could
tell more about its leader than Sun had ever heard before.
Lu believed that Hung had started the rebellion to wipe out
superstition, and all that followed grew out of that first purpose. The two young men liked to discuss superstition, for
they saw it all around them in the life of the village people.
Before long it seemed to them that they ought to attack it.
They began to preach against foot-binding, taking bribes
and smoking opium. The village temple stood more clearly
as a symbol of superstition than anything else. It was so

ancient that its roof was all but falling in, but it had three images, the Northern Emperor, the Queen of Heaven, and the Mother Goddess, and these had recently been freshly decorated. People from the countryside often stopped at the little temple and paid the caretaker a few cents for incense and paper money and candles to burn as offerings before the idols. The young men considered doing something dramatic there.

A festival day came. This was the opportunity they were waiting for. They would attack the problem head on. "Come on," Sun said. "We'll go and observe what they are doing, and then we'll set them straight. We'll have a real audience." As Sun watched the worshippers bowing and burning incense they could not afford, he started to preach against the idols even though he had done just what they were doing when his parents had brought him here as a child.

"I could forgive you if you could give me a single good reason for worshipping these images," he said loudly. "Can they protect you? Do they have strength in their clay arms? Why do you kneel there and burn up good money in candles and incense, when they cannot even protect themselves!"[3] With that Sun stepped up to the nearest image and broke off part of its arm and held it up so that the people could see that it was hollow and stuffed with sacking. Then he went to some of the other idols and mutilated them, too. He looked out over the little crowd in the temple, and those now gathering quickly in the courtyard, before he walked through them and away. Lu had been waiting for him without saying a word. Now he joined him.

"They were holding their breaths, they were so astonished," he said.

"And so afraid," Sun added.

"You had real courage," his friend said admiringly.

The village people had tried to be patient while these young men were preaching to them against foot-binding and taking bribes and smoking opium during the past months, but this affair in the temple was going too far. It was a capital crime under Chinese law to do what they had done and capital punishment could mean decapitation or even being buried alive. Sun was becoming more aware of this every moment. He realized, too, that his father would be blamed for the behavior of his son. The villagers gathered at the Sun house to express their sympathy to the old man. He was not to blame, they said. Yat-sen had been poisoned by Western influences. He was acting madly. In the end it was only because old Mr. Sun was so highly respected that the young man was saved from severe punishment. The decision was that the father was to pay for the repairs of the images and that Sun Yat-sen was to be banished.

Sun did not dare to say how he really felt about his punishment because he was so eager to get away. The months spent in the hopelessly backward village seemed to him to have been wasted. He had wanted to go to school some more in Hawaii and now he thought of studying in Hong Kong. He suggested the idea to his father and his father, anxious to get him away before anything more happened, agreed that Hong Kong might be just the place. He would call a family council and come to a decision. When they met the women cried a little. Sun's father half forgave him although he could never admit it, and he certainly did not understand the young man. What confused the father most of all was how Sun Mei could go to Hawaii and become such a success, and still respect the old family ways, while this boy, under the same circumstances, had become a rebel. The mistake must have been for him to go to that Christian school, Iolani.

4. The Making of a Revolutionist

Iolani had given Sun Yat-sen letters of introduction to an Anglican mission school in Hong Kong before he left the islands and now he got in touch with it. He reached Hong Kong late in the autumn of 1883 and was admitted to the school. The rules of banishment were that one should leave everything he had behind him, but Sun's parents secretly arranged for him to take along a few personal things. Young Sun looked over the British colony with sharp, inquiring eyes. Contrasted with Choyhung, everything seemed smartly efficient. The city administration, the harbor authorities, the modern vehicles, the fine buildings all reminded him of Honolulu.

Sun Yat-sen's father died that winter and this changed everything. Sun had to go home for the proper period of mourning after only a month at school. In April 1884 Sun entered Queen's College in Hong Kong. It was thought of as the best institution there. Now he took rooms with another Chinese on the second floor of a building that was used as a mission day school for boys, and really settled in. An American missionary named Dr. Charles R. Hager occupied part of the third floor of the same building. Sun soon became acquainted with him; the American could not yet speak Chinese but Sun could speak English and they struck up a warm friendship. The mission school and its staff, of which Dr. Hager was one, belonged to the Congregational Church and Sun remembered that it was active in Hawaii, too.

One day Dr. Hager asked Sun Yat-sen whether he was a Christian. He answered that he was a Christian at heart but that he had never been baptized. "Then why don't you be baptized?" the American demanded. "I'm ready any time," Sun told him.[1] Dr. Hager began to prepare the young man for the ceremony. He gave him reading assignments and often quizzed him. In a few months Sun was ready and he was baptized a Christian, a member of the Congregational Church, in a small religious service at the school.

Queen's College was a preparatory school. It had a fine reputation not only for its work in the English language but because it also required education in Chinese scholarship. The two fields had to be kept in balance. No boy who failed in his Chinese work was promoted no matter how well he had done in his English subjects. Sun started in eagerly. Here he could go forward in the best way possible, getting a modern education but also adding to his early training in classical Chinese which he had begun years before in the Choyhung village school.

In several ways 1884 was a big year for Sun Yat-sen. He entered school again, was baptized, and got married. He chose the first two steps but he had no voice in the third. His family arranged for him to be married to a village girl from a family named Lu, on May 7. During the next eight years he would be a student and would rarely see his wife, but the wedding was properly carried out in the old-fashioned style, just the same, and the new daughter-in-law moved to the Sun household and joined his mother and his aunts.

Everything seemed to be going along smoothly now. Sun appeared to be a typical preparatory schoolboy. He wore the long gown and small black skullcap of a student. His shining braid of hair hung down his back and swung with the rhythm of his walking. Only his face was scarcely typical. A photograph shows an unusually vivid, eager expression and large, burning dark eyes. He was scarcely typical, too, because he wanted to get others to join his church. He went on some preaching trips with Dr. Hager and even took the American to his old home. The house was the one Sun Mei had built, better than the others there, and Sun was proud of it even if he would not admit it. Dr. Hager saw Sun's wife although she was so retiring and his ability to speak Chinese so limited that he could not get acquainted with her.

During 1883 and 1884 war broke out between France and China in Annam, now part of Vietnam. China lost Annam to France in the settlement treaty that was drawn up although Annam had been a vassal of China for 2,000 years, since the days of the great unifier, Shih Huang-ti. It was a terrible blow. Sun Yat-sen had a chance to see the meddling of foreign countries at close range, for Annam lay just to the south of Hong Kong. Through the years he would think of Annam many times and be angry again at the Manchus who had failed so completely in protecting China against the white man's aggression. What had happened might not affect his own life, for he wanted to go steadily on with his education now, but he was deeply stirred over what had taken place.

Sun Yat-sen kept on with his work at Queen's College for two years, and then, suddenly, Sun Mei interrupted it. He sent word that his brother was to come to Honolulu at once to sign papers so that the property that was in both their names could be sold. The truth was that Sun Mei had discovered not only that Yat-sen had joined the Church but that he had been going around preaching and trying to make converts. As an older brother Sun Mei had the right to control a younger brother's actions and he was going to put an end to this preaching. Had a protest he had made earlier not reached Yat-sen? If it had, he had paid no attention to it. Now he had to obey Sun Mei's summons. It was true that the brothers were partners and a need to sign papers made sense. Although it was hard to break off in his third year at Queen's, Sun Yat-sen did so and sailed for Hawaii.

When the brothers met they had a stormy quarrel. While it was authentic that papers needed to be signed, Yat-sen soon saw that Sun Mei had wanted him to come primarily to demand that he break all his connections with Christian organizations.

"I'll never do that," the younger man said, his face pale but his eyes blazing. "You have no right to ask it for it is a matter of conviction. I do not ask that you not be a Buddhist, or a follower of any other religion, do I? As your younger brother of course I could not, but were I the older one, I could not feel that it was right to do so."

Sun Mei stared at him. "It is not the same," he answered, "and you know it. This Christianity is not just a private belief. It is like an infection. It changes governments and

politics and trade and all of life. Western nations send out
their missionaries, they say to teach Christianity, but really
they teach revolution—democracy they call it."

He paused and in that moment Sun saw how truly he had
spoken. The teachings of Jesus were revolutionary. The
organization of the church was tied up with politics. He was
interested in the revolutionary teachings and he wanted to
belong to a group that had the same interest.

"If you do not break all of your connections with the
Christians, I shall never give you another penny. You can
find your own passage money back to China," Sun Mei said
through clenched teeth. How could this young brother of
his be so obstinate and so impractical!

Sun Yat-sen turned and left without answering. Sun Mei
always kept his word and he did not want to say things to
his older brother that he would be sorry for later. Yat-sen
went to other Chinese Christians in Honolulu and told them
his problem. Congregational missionaries in the city found
out what had happened, too. They knew that he had done
some preaching back at home and now they suggested that
he return and get training to be a Christian minister. They
collected funds for his passage back and he started out,
going by way of Japan and Shanghai.

All that happened had so interrupted and delayed his
getting back to Hong Kong that he did not arrive there until
the spring of 1886. The school year was ruined. Even
worse, he found that there was no good theological training
school in either Canton or Hong Kong where he could get
the preparation he had agreed to get, nor did he have
money for tuition in any school. For several months he
floundered because he did not know what direction to take.
His best friend during this bad time was Dr. Hager. The

American saw that Yat-sen was still determined about one thing—he was going to get more Western education. The young Chinese firmly believed that he had to lead his country toward progress and that he had to have a modern education to do it.

There seemed to be no possible way to get it except in the field of medicine. China desperately needed Western-trained doctors. Superstition was more damaging to those who were sick than to anyone else. It became clearer and clearer to Sun Yat-sen that he should get a medical training, so he begged Dr. Hager to approach Dr. J. G. Kerr, a Presbyterian medical missionary in Canton who had an outstanding reputation as a surgeon. Dr. Kerr had built up a famous Canton hospital called Pak Tsai. Sun wanted Dr. Hager to find out whether Dr. Kerr would take him on as a student in a medical class that he had been leading for a number of years. There was no medical college to attend and Sun could not think of any other way to get the training he wanted. To the young man's delight Dr. Kerr agreed to take him and also Sun's old "doctrinal friend," Lu, who also wanted to become a doctor.

The two young men roomed together in the Canton Hospital School in the school year 1886–87. They spent their free time discussing China's problems just as they had back in Choyhung. A new step in their thinking developed; they decided that it might not be enough just to denounce the Manchus. Perhaps there would have to be a real revolution to overthrow them. The idea of revolution as the only possible way to bring change took firm root in Sun Yat-sen's mind at this time.

This idea of revolution was strengthened by a third student, named Cheng Shih-liang, who joined them. His father had been a wealthy man but he had failed in a lawsuit and died as a result of it. This young man was full of hatred against all officials, because he felt his father had been treated unjustly by them, and officials were usually Manchus. He was ready to encourage thoughts of revolution and his ideas were helped by the fact that he was a natural leader and an attractive person. One day he told Sun Yat-sen all he knew about secret societies in China, and suggested that they were always helpful in any revolution. Then he confided that he was himself a member of the Triads, that secret society that had helped the Taiping Rebellion.

While the three young men were talking a great deal about revolution, Sun's next step into medicine separated him from the other two, but he kept up a correspondence with his new friend. A way for him to go beyond what Dr. Kerr could teach him had developed, for a new medical school was starting in Hong Kong in connection with the Alice Memorial Hospital. It was being established by still another church group, the London Missionary Society, and was to open in October 1887. One of the doctors in the British community in Hong Kong closely connected with the new institution was a Dr. James Cantlie. The first student who came to register was Sun Yat-sen. No one knew where the eager young man got the money for his tuition and his expenses although he was known to have a wealthy brother in Hawaii. If Sun Mei had forgiven him and decided to help him as long as he was going to be a doctor rather than a preacher, he kept the matter to himself.

Sun threw himself into his studies wholeheartedly, for he thoroughly enjoyed them. He got to know Dr. Cantlie well and the two of them began a long friendship. Sun could also discuss revolution with other young Chinese quite safely here in the British colony, and he and three others were soon nicknamed the Four Big Brigands. Sun went even further and joined the Triad secret society. During his first year at the medical school, too, his wife gave birth to a son, whom he named Sun Fo.

After five years of study, the young doctor graduated, the first to graduate as he had been the first to register. He was twenty-seven and ready to start a practice once he could locate a place.

During his years of preparation he had gone back and forth to Macao a good many times because he and his friends were carrying on some revolutionary activities there. They had organized themselves into the Revive China Society or the Hsin Chung Hui. These contacts with Macao now made Sun Yat-sen think of it as a place where he might be able to start a medical practice. If this plan worked out he could be revolutionist and physician at the same time. He looked around for a location and found an old-fashioned Chinese hospital where they allowed him the use of one building for a surgery. Dr. Cantlie was so interested in his pupil's success that he often made the long boat trip from Hong Kong to Macao to help him, although it took hours. He hardly knew himself why he went on these time-consuming journeys except that he loved and respected Sun Yat-sen. The young man had a magnetic charm that attracted more and more loyal friends. The British physician was astonished at the way Sun could perform operations surrounded by the curious members of the patients' families and under the eye of the Chinese hospital's managing committee, which seated itself around the operating table. The audience was particularly interested in watching Dr. Sun remove gallstones from a patient.

Sun's practice did well until the authorities of the Portuguese colony enforced a regulation which required a Portuguese medical diploma from anyone carrying on a practice there. When this happened, Sun moved to Canton. In this large city he set up two offices, one in the city itself and the other in its outskirts. Soon both of them were also used for political work. His old friend Lu Hao-tung came to help with this. While Sun was a skilled surgeon and physician, his thoughts were more and more on the political situation of his country. Years later he confided in his autobiography, "All the years between 1885 and 1895 were like a day in my hard fight for national liberty, and my medical practice was no more to me than a means of introducing my propaganda to the world."[2]

Although the practice in Canton was going well, in the summer of 1893 he and his friend Lu decided to look for a position in the north. Sun had heard that the elderly but famous viceroy Li Hung-chang, who was trying to bring about a gradual modernizing of China by setting up new educational institutions, planned to open a medical college in Tientsin, just south of Peking. Sun and his friend went north, thinking that they might be able to get jobs in this new college and dreaming of meeting the viceroy and presenting him with a political proposal in the form of a memorial or petition.

The two men labored hard over this memorial, trying to avoid any statement that might seem too radical, and emphasizing such changes as free public schools, the application of science to farming methods, more use of natural resources, and better transportation and industrialization.

This was the first time Sun Yat-sen had set down the things he believed in and the things he would work for—his declaration of independence. He would do it again and again. While the statement certainly described broad goals and they were unquestionably good ones, the two young men who tried to present it to the viceroy never saw him. They could not even get anyone in Peking to accept their memorial for him. They were crestfallen and discouraged.

But now that they were in the capital they decided to see it and try to discover how tightly the Manchus held power. After they had taken as much time for this as they wanted, they returned to Canton slowly, visiting two important sister cities, Wuchang and Hankow, which stood 650 miles inland from Shanghai on the Yangtze River, and talking with all kinds of people as they went.

When they finally reached Canton once more it was summer 1894. They found that war was about to break out between China and Japan over the control of Korea. They had had hints of this in Peking, too, but now the situation had grown worse. Sun was sure that China would lose to Japan because Japan had much greater military strength. It was certainly not a good time to attempt revolution in China herself and he decided he would not try it. Instead, he sailed for Hawaii to see if he could build up more support for change among overseas Chinese. He believed that revolution lay ahead, although that revolution was still vague in his thinking. It would clearly have to be against the old dynastic government of China, and for a new democratic form of organization. Surely, he thought, Chinese living abroad under democratic governments would be more than ready to support such a change in their own homeland.

II. ORGANIZING REVOLUTION

5 Spreading the "Revive China Society"

After Sun Yat-sen had left China for Honolulu, his memorial to Viceroy Li Hung-chang was published in a Shanghai journal that many educated Chinese read. It was the first time that important intellectual leaders found out much about his revolutionary thinking. Years later some of them said that had the viceroy received the two young men with their petition, the future history of China might have been very different from what it was. Sun might have been kept from giving up hope of changing the situation by peaceful measures, as he did when he could not even present his carefully prepared statement.

Now as he neared Hawaii he came to have one clear purpose. He was going to set up a worldwide organization based on the Revive China Society (Hsin Chung Hui) which he had begun in Macao. This organization would be dedicated to the overthrow of the Manchu Dynasty, and to the establishment of a new government.

When he reached Honolulu and went to see Sun Mei,

all the old quarrel was forgotten. To his astonishment Sun
Mei even joined the branch of the Revive China Society that
was formed there and persuaded some other wealthy busi-
nessmen to become members also. Sun was very much encouraged by this and he went all over the islands starting new
chapters of his society. These overseas Chinese pledged
themselves to work together to modernize China. They sent
statement after statement to Peking, but no one knew if any
of them were read, for no reply ever came back. This failure to get response increased the discontent of the overseas
Chinese. The Revive China Society grew so quickly in
Hawaii that it was soon clear that its organization had to be
improved. It was decided that its headquarters had to be in
China, best of all in Shanghai, and that members would
raise funds by buying ten-dollar shares.

While Sun Yat-sen was in Honolulu he received a letter
from an old friend of his in Shanghai. Soong Yao-ju, or
Charlie Soong, was a merchant who as a boy had been sent
to his uncle, who had a silk and tea shop in Boston. He had
run away from there and had been taken aboard the S.S.
Colfax, which plied between Boston and Savannah. The
cutter's captain, Charles Jones, was kind-hearted even if he
was sometimes gruff. He was interested in the Chinese boy
and put him in touch with the pastor of a Methodist church
in Wilmington, North Carolina, one of their ports of call, in
1880. Through this contact Charlie had become a member
of the Church and been baptized with the captain's first
name, sent to a Church school and then to one of its theological seminaries. He had returned to Shanghai with the
idea of becoming a pastor, but he had soon given that up to
go into business. Charlie Soong had married well and he
and his wife had become prominent citizens of the great

city. By the time Sun Yat-sen had become acquainted with Charlie Soong, many years had passed and he had five children. But even when he had been a boy in America Charlie Soong had thought about the problem of modernizing China. Now he was ready to support Sun Yat-sen in every way he could. The letter Sun received from his old friend urged him to return to China at once and start a revolution. Things were going so badly in the war now being fought with Japan that Soong thought this was the moment to introduce revolution as a hope for the people.

Sun Yat-sen had been planning to go on to America from Hawaii, to set up more chapters of the Revive China Society and to collect more funds. Now, because of Soong's letter he changed his plans and returned to China, taking some of his leaders with him. Soon after he got back the war with Japan ended with the Treaty of Shimonoseki, signed April 17, 1895, in which China recognized the independence of Korea, and gave Japan Formosa. Everyone knew that the so-called independent Korea would soon be Japan's, too. The atmosphere was charged with anger and outrage.

Confusion in China mounted as warlords claimed large areas, fighting each other in private contests to get all they could. Soldiers who had been marshaled against Japan now wandered over the countryside as bandits. Small rebellions broke out here and there for no one seemed to be in control.

Sun Yat-sen and his men felt that China had been disgraced in her defeat by Japan. Perhaps Charlie Soong was right in thinking now was the time for action. They began to lay careful and secret plans to take over the Manchu government in Canton because revolutionary feeling was strong there. The revolutionary organization which they set up in Canton was called the Scientific Agricultural Association to disguise its real nature. Sun's old friend, Lu Hao-tung, was at the head of it. The revolutionists opened a branch office in Hong Kong also, using a store as a front. They began to recruit men secretly, engaged some American chemists to manufacture bombs, and bought dynamite and other arms from the Philippines. They also organized a network of men who belonged to their society to handle the shipping of military goods. Their spies found out how the Manchu officials worked so that their whereabouts on a certain day or at a certain hour were predictable. The conspirators invented secret signals. Lu Hao-tung designed a revolutionary flag with five bars running its full length, meaning the unity of all China's original peoples. He told the tailor who was making it that it was a quilt for his sister's bed. To the revolutionists it meant change from the Dragon Throne symbol of monarchy to democracy under a republic, and the young men in Canton began to work feverishly to bring that change about.

The fateful day for the first attempt at revolution was set for September 9, 1895. Sun Yat-sen was not in Canton but in a secret hideout in the province. The city's Manchu government was to be seized first and this was to set off a chain of events. On September 8 five columns of men took their places on a road leading into the city according to plan. Another detachment was due to come from Hong Kong. By early the next morning it had still not arrived. A shipment of 600 rifles was supposed to be aboard a Chinese ship hidden in barrels of cement, but now the shipment could not be located. Sun Yat-sen hurriedly sent word to Hong Kong to try to cancel the plan if it had not been begun so that it would not be discovered, but he found it could not now be stopped. The Maritime Customs in Canton soon discovered the rifles hidden in cement on a ship, for a traitor had given away the secret. Now the revolutionary headquarters were raided and seventy men were arrested. One of them was Lu Hao-tung, who had been trying to escape when he remembered that the membership list of the Revive China Society and other important papers had been left behind. He turned back to burn the papers and in that short time imperial troops surrounded the place and arrested him. When Christian friends found out what had happened they tried desperately to defend him, but he was too proud to accept mercy from the Manchu officials whom he had been planning to destroy. He and three others were executed, the first martyrs of the Chinese Revolution. The crew of the ship that had been involved in transporting arms were also arrested, their officers were shot and the men were thrown into jail where they were allowed slowly to starve to death.

Sun Yat-sen's friends hid him and he did not dare to make a move for several days. Then he set out for Macao by way of Canton. He was so well known in that city that no one would expect him to try to go there. He traveled by several different methods changing from one to another when he thought it safer. Once when he was riding in a closed sedan chair and the police asked his chair coolies if they knew where he was, he was delighted to hear them say that although they knew where a Dr. Yin lived, they had no idea about any Dr. Sun. He knew that these laboring men were defending him because they were members of secret societies and they had found out about his own secret society that was dedicated to changing China.

It took him ten days to reach Canton. He stayed with a

friend on the outskirts of the city for a night and during the darkness revolutionists helped him down over the city wall, for city gates were always closed at dusk. Once inside the city he made his way to the home of his friend of Canton Hospital School days, Cheng Shih-liang. Now they set out together for Macao, having to hide themselves all the way. They went along creeks and canals in any boat that would take them, and when soldiers came to search the boats for refugees who might be rebels, they disappeared into the marshland of the shores. When at last they came to Macao Sun found the public places plastered with posters announcing a reward of approximately $15,000 for his capture. He went on to Hong Kong as quickly as he could.

In Hong Kong Sun searched out his old friend and teacher, Dr. Cantlie, who was alarmed because of the danger Sun was in. "I'll send you to my lawyer," he said anxiously. "Do whatever he advises." Sun went reluctantly.

"You'll have to leave the country as quickly as you can," the lawyer said. "Otherwise you will certainly be arrested, and . . ." He did not need to finish. Sun and two of his men took ship for Kobe, Japan, their passages paid by friends.

Aboard ship there was time to think. "From now on I am a marked man," Sun told himself. "I am a political criminal." Even though he recognized this fact, he was not prepared to see posters offering rewards for his capture wherever the ship docked. Not only had the attempt at revolution failed, its leader was helpless and important people who had not been in full sympathy with so drastic a move as seizing the government in Canton were now ready to criticize.

In escaping, Sun Yat-sen had not been able to shave for some time. The border of hair around his queue which the barber normally shaved when his hair was rebraided had also had time to grow a good deal. He looked at himself in a mirror and decided on a big step. As soon as he came to a barbershop in Kobe he went in and had his queue cut off, his hair trimmed and his face shaved, leaving a moustache. When he looked into the mirror again he was amazed at how different he was. Now he could disquise himself quite easily. When he found a clothing store he went in and bought a Western-style suit like most Japanese men were wearing to work every day. He studied himself in a mirror again. His skin was like his mother's, a little darker than that of the average Chinese of South China. With his modern haircut, moustache, and new suit, he would easily pass as a Japanese.

Cutting off his queue seemed to Sun a milestone. For so long he had refused to do it unless it could be done by many as a sign that they were throwing off the domination of the Manchus who had required this hairdress. He had dreamed of a day when the Chinese people would cut their long hair off in a dramatic declaration of freedom. Now Sun saw that the times demanded that he declare himself as forever against the Manchus, without any further delay. He must be the leader of the revolution, and as that leader he could no longer wear a badge indicating that he was a servant of the aggressor. Danger as well as the facts of history had forced him to this decision. He stepped out into the Kobe streets, a short, darkish man with heavy black hair that was neatly combed and a small moustache, dressed in a business suit with a bright tie. No one looked at him twice.

There was nothing he could do now except let time pass. People had to forget about him and stop trying to find him. He gave one of his friends a post in connection with the Revive China Society in Japan, and sent the other back to

China. After a time he went on to Hawaii secretly and Sun Mei took him in.

When Choyhung village heard of all that had happened to Sun Yat-sen, the people became excited and were terribly afraid. Members of Sun's family and Lu's family, who were still there, believed that they might be in danger because of what Sun Yat-sen and Lu Hao-tung had done, even though Lu was now dead. His terrible end only made them more fearful. It happened that a young man of the Lu family who had gone to Hawaii was at this time in Choyhung again, looking for a bride to take back with him. When the full news of what Sun had tried to do in Canton reached Sun Mei, now sheltering Yat-sen, the older brother hastily arranged for the young Lu man to escort old Mrs. Sun, Yat-sen's wife and the three children they now had, Sun Fo and two younger girls, to him in Hawaii. All this seemed like panic action to Sun Yat-sen until word came that the father of the young bridegroom who had escorted the Sun family to Hawaii had been arrested and thrown into jail. The son sent almost $6,000 to try to get his father released but this was not accomplished until six years later when China's foreign minister in Washington succeeded in getting the release.

"Sun Mei is still the dutiful son," Sun Yat-sen thought to himself. He felt no jealousy for his older brother, who had given up rice farming to become a cattle-raiser in the island of Maui. It did not seem unusual when Sun Mei took in all the family and relatives, permanently, for this fitted in with the old Chinese tradition. Whenever Yat-sen saw his wife and children during the next years, it was at Sun Mei's home. The arrangement left him free to go on with the revolution.

But for a long time Sun did not know what his next step ought to be. Since he could not do anything in the Far East, he finally decided he would go to America and then possibly on to England. The groups of overseas Chinese everywhere ought to be enlisted to help the cause.

One day before he left Hawaii, when he was in Honolulu on business, he caught sight of Dr. and Mrs. Cantlie, his old friends from Hong Kong, walking with their small son and his Japanese nursemaid. Dr. Sun raised his hat and hailed them joyfully, but they only stared back at him without a sign of recognition. At last the puzzled nursemaid addressed him in Japanese, thinking that he must be a fellow national. When he introduced himself in English the Cantlies could scarcely get over their surprise, for they had been completely deceived by his disguise. Dr. Cantlie had not heard a word of what had happened since the day Sun Yatsen had visited the lawyer in Hong Kong. Now they spent the time they had together seeing Honolulu and planned to see each other again in London.

Dr. Sun sailed for San Francisco in June, 1896. He managed to disembark without trouble even though the Geary Exclusion Act against Oriental immigrants was in force against Chinese and would have been expected to affect him. He may have entered as a Japanese. In any case he spent a month in San Francisco and felt so confident of his disguise that he even sat for a fine photograph of himself. When he started across the continent he did it in a leisurely way, stopping to talk to groups of Chinese wherever he could find them. He explained the crisis in China and emphasized the need for a complete reconstruction of the government and the economy. But only a few were really interested in what he said. He could count them in a few dozen.

While he was traveling in this way, the Chinese Minister in Washington discovered that he was in the United States. He even secured copies of the photograph that Dr. Sun had had taken. The Minister kept informed of Dr. Sun's itinerary, and when he sailed from New York for Liverpool on the S.S. *Majestic* on September 23, the Minister cabled the information to the Chinese Minister in London, giving details of Dr. Sun's work against the Chinese government and calling him a political criminal. He said that as a revolutionist Dr. Sun should be watched and that the British government ought to be asked to extradite him, or return him to China, because he was dangerous.

When he arrived in London on October 1, Dr. Sun innocently put up at Haxell's Hotel in the Strand and the next day went to see the Cantlies. They said that he was too far away from them and found him a lodging nearer to them; they saw each other often from then on. One time when they were out walking Dr. Cantlie laughingly pointed out the Chinese embassy, which was not far from Dr. Sun's rooms, and jokingly suggested that he might make a call there. Mrs. Cantlie said quickly that it was not a laughing matter and warned Dr. Sun to stay away from the place, or they might catch him and ship him back to China.

Dr. Sun happily enjoyed London for ten days, with no idea that he was being watched. Sometimes he read in Dr. Cantlie's study. Often he and the Cantlies went out together. Then one Sunday morning when Dr. Sun was on his way to meet his British friends and go to church with them, a Chinese man suddenly appeared at his side and asked him whether he was Chinese or Japanese. When Dr. Sun replied that he was Chinese, the man began to talk in a very friendly fashion, asking what province Dr. Sun was from, and when he learned it was Kwangtung said that that, too, was his home province. At this moment a second Chinese man appeared, and suddenly Dr. Sun found himself being escorted into a large pillared building. He was given a tour of the place, Chinese porcelains and other fine items were pointed out to him, and then he was whisked to a room on the third floor. The two men who had brought him here disappeared, the door was closed behind them, and locked. Dr. Sun turned to see a gray-haired English gentleman confronting him. This man, Sir Halliday Macartney, explained that this was the Chinese legation and that he was English adviser to the legation. He said that word had come from China that Dr. Sun would be arriving in London and that he should be watched as a political criminal. He addressed Dr. Sun most politely but he ended, "You will have to remain under the legation's custody in this building until we receive instructions from Peking," and left the room. A Chinese guard was already stationed at the door.

Dr. Sun was frantic. When he discovered later that the man who had accosted him outdoors and who had claimed to be from Canton was the legation interpreter, they had a long discussion of the arrest. The interpreter let slip the information that the legation was trying to find a way to ship Dr. Sun back to China. This made the prisoner feel even worse, for he knew that if the legation succeeded, in its plan it would cost him his life, and Manchu methods of punishing political prisoners were famous for their cruelty.

As hour passed hour and then day passed day, he tried desperately to think what to do. If only he could get in touch with the Cantlies! Why did they not know? Was there nothing in the newspapers? He could not answer his own questions. He wrote letters to his friends but when no reply

came he felt sure that they were never received in spite of
the money he gave the servant to deliver them. He wrote
notes, weighted them with coins and dropped them from his
windows when no one was watching, hoping that some
passerby would get his appeal and send help. Nothing happened; much later he found that they had lodged on an out-
jutting roof and had never reached the street below as he
had intended. Soon he saw no one from one day to the next
except the English servants who brought him food and
tended the fire in his chilly room.

He could not sleep, he could not eat; he was in a state of
panic. At last on one desperate day he begged the servant
who brought in coal to listen to him. He told the man that
the Emperor of China wanted to execute him simply because as a Christian he was trying to get a better government for his country. He said that he had important British
friends who would stand by him if only he could get word
of his predicament to them. "My life is in your hands," he
told the servant. "If you let the matter be known outside, I
shall be saved; if not, I shall certainly be executed."[1] When
Dr. Sun put it this way, the appeal was too strong for the
man to resist. He hid a note to the Cantlies in his coal
scuttle and carried it out.

Late on the night of October 17 someone rang Dr. Cantlie's doorbell and pushed a letter under the door. The messenger had disappeared by the time the doctor answered the
door. The letter said, "There is a friend of yours imprisoned
in the Chinese legation here since last Sunday; they intend
sending him out to China, where it is certain they will hang
him. It is very sad for the poor young man, and unless
something is done at once he will be taken away and no one
will know it. I dare not sign my name, but this is the truth,

so believe what I say. Whatever you do must be done at once, or it will be too late. His name is, I believe, Sin Yin Sen."[2] This was not the note that Dr. Sun had sent out, but a letter prepared by the English servant's wife. Perhaps this explains the strange spelling of his name.

Dr. Cantlie did not even wait until morning to start. He tried to reach the English adviser of the Chinese legation even though by now it was midnight. He failed. He set out immediately for Scotland Yard. Scotland Yard declared that no existing law made it legal for the British police to get into such an affair.

The next morning, now a week since Dr. Sun had been kidnapped, Dr. Cantlie went to ask the help of Sir Patrick Manson, who had been one of Dr. Sun's professors at the Alice Memorial Hospital in Hong Kong. At Manson's door Dr. Cantlie found the English servant who was helping Dr. Sun. He had some visiting cards on which Dr. Sun had written notes about his desperate situation. One said, "I was kidnapped on Sunday last by two Chinamen, and forcibly taken into the Chinese legation. I am imprisoned, and in a day or two I am to be shipped off to China on board a specially chartered vessel. I am certain to be beheaded. Oh, woe is me!"[3] The two doctors went on to Scotland Yard but were again refused any help there. They did not waste any more time but found a private detective firm. It posted a watch on the Chinese legation and then went to the offices of the *Times* and made a public statement on what had happened. But the story was not published for several days, until it was too late to help.

Dr. Cantlie pushed on. The next day, which was Monday, he went to the British Foreign Office where he found that word had already come that a ship had been chartered

to take Dr. Sun back to China. Later the public would find
out that the Peking government had authorized spending up
to $6,000 to secure him. The British Foreign Office advised
Scotland Yard to keep a close watch. Meantime a writ of
habeas corpus against the Chinese legation was prepared
but the judge of Old Bailey refused to allow it to be served.
Dr. Cantlie was frustrated at everything he tried. Tuesday
and Wednesday had passed by now. All that was left was
public opinion.

On Thursday morning Dr. Cantlie decided to use public
opinion as a last resort. The *Times* story had still not been
used. He gave the *Globe* a long interview and that evening
the home-going crowds read the headlines, "Chinese Revolutionary Kidnapped in London!" People rushed toward the
Chinese legation. Dr. Cantlie drove up in a hansom cab.
The English adviser to the legation was located. Dr. Cantlie
and the British Secretary of Foreign Affairs had a conference, and then the Secretary informed the Chinese Minister
that imprisonment without trial was not permitted by British common law. He advised the Minister to release Dr. Sun
at once.

When the word spread, people began to gather excitedly
below the building where Dr. Sun was imprisoned. On the
third floor he could hear the hubbub in the street below but
he had no idea what it was. The next day, twelve days after
he had been imprisoned, he was released. When he stepped
out he was astonished at the welcome the waiting people
gave him. The crowds followed him to his hotel and news-
men pressed him for a story. He was already exhausted by
anxiety; when the friendly visitors continued to come all
night and through the next day, Dr. Cantlie finally begged
them to let the doctor rest.

Dr. Sun had experienced more than just imprisonment. He had gone through a time when he had had to think about his religion and his real purposes. Many years later he wrote of his experience as God-given. He knew now that he was wholly committed to the revolution, whatever it might cost. He had escaped what had seemed to be an inescapable situation, he believed, with God's help. From now on he would trust a guidance beyond himself because he had come to the conclusion that Heaven was ordering his life. For centuries the Chinese had held that there was such a thing as holding a mandate from Heaven. Sun Yat-sen was convinced that he held that mandate now.

6. No Compromise

Now that he was free, Sun Yat-sen asked himself what his next step ought to be. He thought of going back to China, but strange things were happening there. Two reformers were attempting to change China by dramatic reforms rather than by revolution, reminding him of the memorial he had tried to give the viceroy. Their names were Kang Yu-wei and Liang Chi-chao. The young Emperor welcomed ideas that would improve his country although the powerful Empress Dowager was hostile to them. Schools that taught Western subjects were opened, the army was being reformed and a naval college had been proposed. Western textbooks were being translated into Chinese. Although a new day really seemed to be on the way, even to Dr. Sun, he was troubled by the fact that foreign powers were involved in many of these changes. Railroad and mining concessions were being offered to them in the hope of getting modernization more quickly than if the Chinese did it themselves. Russia had secured railroad rights in Manchuria, France and Belgium had rights for a line connecting Peking and Hankow, while Germany was proposing a line in Shantung Province. Dr. Sun was especially interested in China's transportation, for he saw it as a key to much of her future development.

Now he heard and read all the news about these plans that were being made, and as he thought things over it seemed to him that the reformers were really his enemies, for they were strengthening the empire rather than over-throwing it. They were trying to cure things from the top down when he believed that the change had to come from the roots up.

Still, he took time to think it all over. He went to the reading room of the British Museum in London and began to study political theories, economics and sociology. During long lonely hours there he came to have a clearer idea of what basic revolution really was. He had been dreaming of quick results. Now he saw that it would take much longer than he had thought and he wondered whether he could be that patient.

One day some Russian exiles came into the library and he soon discovered that they, too, were interested in revolution. As they talked together they compared their hopes for their countries. It was discouraging to find that the Russians also thought that revolution would take a much longer time to prove successful than he had been estimating.

At last Dr. Sun was so restless that he could no longer stay in London. He went to the Continent and wandered about, discouraged and lonely, for he did not dare to go near legations and he could not find many Chinese students. He had practically no money so he traveled on foot and spent just as little on food and lodging as he possibly could.

Still, he was having a chance to observe democratic governments at work, and he was astonished to see that even
under democracies people could be dissatisfied. Some of
them were talking about socialist revolution or about
changing the economic systems of their countries in some
other way. He himself began to consider socialism.

A day came when Dr. Sun could not wait any longer to
start for China. In 1898 he returned to London and sailed
for Canada and the United States. From the United States he
set out for Japan, stopping in Hawaii to see his family and
posing for pictures with them. Dr. Sun knew that he could
not go to Hong Kong for the Chinese Minister in London
had asked the British Foreign Office to make sure that their
foreign colony was not again used as a base for revolution.
But Japan would be safe because China had no special
rights over Chinese living there; these had been taken away
at the end of China's war with Japan. Chinese in Japan
were just treated like any other foreigners. Now he set sail
for Yokohama. There members of the Japanese Liberal
Party were waiting to welcome him and take him on to the
capital, Tokyo, where he had a friendly meeting with a
large group of them. Back in Yokohama, Dr. Sun found a
place to live in the foreign section of the city, and set up his
office for the revolution. He believed that there must be as
many as 10,000 Chinese in Japan and he thought that he
would find a strong support for his plans among them.

This was the third time that Dr. Sun had been in Japan.
The first was when he had stopped there on his return to
China from Hawaii when he was eighteen years old. The
second was when he escaped from China after the first try
at the revolution. That was when he cut his queue and
changed his appearance. Now it was 1899.

As he started in on the job of laying new plans, he was amused to discover that his office was almost next door to the Chinese consulate, or diplomatic offices, which only a few years earlier would have had legal power to arrest and execute him for his revolutionary activities. Well, the war with Japan had had one good result, anyway. Now he worked along quite complacently knowing that no authority could touch him, legally. Some of his friends were not so comfortable. They were always warning him that he might be attacked by an assassin hired to do the job by an enemy of his ideas. They watched over him, but he would not have a bodyguard.

When he started actual organization for the revolution, he could see clearly what his problems were. He would have to disassociate his movement from that of the reformers who were working on changes but still acknowledging the greatness of the past and the good points of the Manchu government. The reformers had a student following just as he had, but they were students of China's ancient arts and literature, not those who had been educated in Western schools and been bitten by new ideas. His followers had long ago given up hope of what they wanted for their country under the old form of government and had attached themselves to the revolution. The fact that so many of the "intellectuals" had swung to the reform group made those students who did not want to be in that classification swing to the revolutionary organization, too.

Members of secret societies, some of which had begun as loyalty groups, or those loyal to the earlier non-Manchu dynasties, also became followers of Dr. Sun. He himself had joined the Triad Society earlier and he had formed his own secret society, the Revive China Society, or Hsin Chung

Hui. Now from Japan he began to see that his greatest support might lie in secret societies and he wanted to bring them together and unify them.

At the very time he was thinking of this plan seriously, one of the secret societies in China, called the Corps of Righteous Harmony or Boxers, broke out into fierce hostility against foreign powers which were so involved in the programs of the reform groups. The Empress Dowager, who was still enormously powerful in spite of the young Emperor's authority, was famous for her hatred of foreigners. She supported the Boxers even though they used many ridiculously superstitious methods in their fighting. When the foreign powers protested strongly against their nationals being attacked by the Boxers, the Empress sent a prominent leader of the Imperial Army to stop them to keep up appearances to the foreigners, for she was still secretly on the side of the Boxers.

Dr. Sun watched this rebellion from Japan with great interest. An entire garrison of the Imperial Army went over to the Boxers and besieged the foreign settlement in Tientsin. Foreign ships attacked the Taku Forts, which guarded the sea approach to the city. The railroad between Peking and Tientsin was cut and the capital was in turmoil. Twenty-three Christians were killed, the German Minister and then the Chancellor of the Japanese legation were murdered. Foreigners in Peking were held like prisoners. At the end of a terrible summer international troops entered the city and finally freed them, the court fled and the city was looted. Now the foreign powers demanded a settlement. Dr. Sun guessed that it would be more than a settlement, it would be punishment. After trying to find some way of avoiding the harsh terms that China was offered, the Empress accepted

them in December 1900. Besides punishing the individual
leaders who had been involved, China would have to pay a
huge fine or indemnity, finance the legations' guards, repay
the cost of the buildings that had been destroyed, and repair
forts used by foreign troops. Where foreign cemeteries had
been desecrated, monuments of apology would have to be
erected. When Dr. Sun heard of this, it was almost more
than he could bear. What the foreigners really wanted to do
was humiliate China. She had been humiliated before but
she had never been asked to repay so much. All this was
only another sign of the terrible condition his country was
in, a condition he hoped to change.

One step forward now seemed possible. Li Hung-chang,
the viceroy he had wanted to see in Peking five years earlier, was now leading two southern provinces, one of them
Sun's own, in an independence movement. Evidently he
had grown impatient, too. Sun heard a rumor that Li
wanted him to come and act as an adviser. It sounded unlikely, but Sun could not afford to miss any chance that
might help in promoting his cause. He quickly sent one of
his men to approach Li Hung-chang and find out whether
what he had heard was true while he sailed to Saigon, by
way of Hong Kong. His man reported that the rumor was
false, for Li had already returned to Peking.

On board ship returning from Saigon to Hong Kong, Dr.
Sun held a military conference with the men who had accompanied him. He decided that the time had come to start
a second attempt at revolution. He would have to become a
military strategist and have arms and men to do this and he
put his mind on meeting these needs.

They would make the town of Waichow, which was
about 100 miles east of Canton on the East River, their

center. Sun dispatched one of his leaders there, two more to Canton, and a fourth to assume responsibility for arms, ammunition and supplies. Sun planned to go ashore in Hong Kong and stay there while he tried to collect a foreign militia and move them to Waichow secretly. But the British had not forgotten the London incident and now they would not permit him to disembark in Hong Kong. He had to return to Saigon. There he discovered that one of his men had been jailed on false charges in Singapore. He hurried to that city and succeeded in getting the man released. Then, because Hong Kong was closed to him, he decided to go to Formosa. Since the end of the war between Japan and China it had been under Japan's control and he would have no problems. The Japanese governor of Formosa was in sympathy with Dr. Sun's plans and made Japanese experts available to him. Dr. Sun also bought Japanese arms and, discovering that the Philippines had ammunition left from their attempt at revolution in 1898, he ordered a large amount from them.

Dr. Sun's plans expanded. He dreamed of being able to capture the seacoasts of two adjacent provinces, that of his own, Kwangtung, and that of Fukien. If he succeeded in this, he believed that it would be possible for the revolutionists to seize the important mainland port, Amoy, which was just across the Formosan Straits. He put Cheng Shih-liang, the old school friend who had become an outstanding revolutionary leader, in charge of the operation. One city after another along the coast fell. But the ammunition supply was held up somewhere. Cheng's forces had to fall back because of it, and in the end were defeated. Then Japan's government changed, turning conservative. Help that the friendly governor of Formosa had promised was cancelled, with the result that Cheng had to discharge his army. In Canton the revolutionists were ordered to blow up the *yamen* as soon as they got word that Cheng and what was left of his troops were coming so as to cooperate with him and still accomplish something, but the explosion was so small that the revolutionist in charge of the attempt was captured and killed while the Manchu viceroy was not even hurt. Sun Yat-sen went to Japan to think over the failure of the second attempt at revolution. He was discouraged but he tried to make every failure a learning experience. He even told some of his men that now they could see how easily the imperial troops could be defeated if they were attacked by well-trained revolutionists.

A group of followers were beginning to gather around Dr. Sun as time passed because he could explain the meaning of Western culture to them, and he decided to stay on in Japan for a year to encourage this exchange of ideas. Young people in both Japan and China wanted what he had to give because he had had a Western education and had been abroad although he was still a Chinese scholar and devoted to his own country. His reputation spread beyond his own immediate group and many came to listen to what he had to say.

While this was going on Dr. Sun began to hear about something that was happening on the mainland. In his small Yokahama office he learned that the reform movement was deepening and expanding. Although the Chinese court was still in exile, shamed by the Boxer Rebellion, it knew that some steps to modernize China had to be taken without delay. The educational system was being reorganized and the old-fashioned methods of writing compositions were abolished, modern schools were planned, and students were

encouraged to go abroad to study. Some new universities
had been opened at the end of the war with Japan and now
more of them were planned. Mission schools were suddenly
flooded with applicants who wanted Western education.
Young men throughout the countryside who had for gener-
ations attended village schools and then gone up for the
civil service examinations, now were to be provided with
Western training.

Students from China also started to flood Japan where
they could get the education they wanted, and then went on
to the West if they had the money to do so. Sun watched
this trickle grow into a steady stream; many of these students came to find him and crowded around to hear what
he had to say. Although as time passed he became more and
more blunt in what he was stating and writing, he main-
tained a curious personal magnetism that was highly attractive.

One of China's active reformers, the Liang Chi-chao
mentioned earlier, came to Japan, too, and he and Dr. Sun
met and tried to find some basis of agreement. It was impossible; Liang was still for reforming the monarchy, while Sun
was dedicated to overthrowing it by revolution. The talks
with Liang only made Dr. Sun more determined on his own
course. But he did start to think of the power of the press in
a new way, for Liang was an outstanding writer for the
Chinese papers. Before long Dr. Sun was quoted as saying,
"One newspaper is worth a hundred thousand soldiers." To
bear it out he sent some of his men to Hong Kong to start
the *Chung Kuo Pao* or *China News,* which soon became the
mouthpiece of the revolutionists.

It was fine to sit and sip tea with the reformer Liang, and
to discuss reform versus revolution in polite terms, but

when Dr. Sun discovered that the reform movement was spreading among Chinese in Hawaii, which he thought of as the birthplace of his revolution, he wrote a strong letter to his countrymen there. He pointed out that that movement was planning to put the young Emperor back on the throne. He wrote even more excitedly to Chinese in the United States and begged them to be alert to what was about to happen. "If only I could come and explain things to you, you would soon be convinced," he declared.

He reached a point where he could not wait around in Japan any longer. In 1903, after he had been there for more than two years, he made up his mind to start on a second world tour to rally revolutionaries and to raise funds for yet another attempt to overthrow the monarchy.

7. Establishing a New Political Party

Dr. Sun's plan for a second world tour was delayed by a rather unusual event. An exposition was to take place in Hanoi, Annam, a French possession since China's war with France, and the French legation in Tokyo invited Dr. Sun to attend it. He accepted because such an occasion would give him an opportunity to meet important French officials; whether he approved of their colonial rule or not, he needed their help. He would get acquainted with many wealthy Chinese living in Southeast Asia, too. When he went to Hanoi things worked out just as he hoped. Important Chinese joined the Revive China Society and made large contributions to it.

That autumn of 1903, when the exposition was over, Dr. Sun started on his world tour, sailing for Honolulu. There he was happy to find that his family was doing well under Sun Mei's guardianship. Sun Fo, the oldest child, was twelve now and Dr. Sun was proud of his progress in school. The two little girls were full of fun and excitement when they welcomed their father. Dr. Sun called the members of the Revive China Society together in Honolulu. Even though he heard that many overseas Chinese favored reform rather than revolution, he was warmly supported. When he held a public meeting in the Hotel Street Theater the building was crowded. All who came were Chinese and most of them still wore their traditional dress; Dr. Sun's modern appearance contrasted with that of his audience. They were soon caught by his magnetism, yet later some of them described him as a serious, balanced speaker, not an extremist or a fanatic. "He is devoting his life to arousing a spirit of nationalism among us," they said, "for he firmly believes that once this spirit is aroused Chinese everywhere will rise up and overthrow the Manchu government." Dr. Sun was encouraged, but he also realized that his enemy, the reform movement, was not dying. Again and again he came up against the eloquent writings of Liang Chi-chao.

On March 31, 1904, Dr. Sun sailed for the United States on the S.S. *Korea*. This time he had an American passport. His birthplace had been reported as Hawaii in a Hong Kong newspaper in 1896, the year he entered the United States the first time, passing as a Japanese. Then it had been printed in a book about the London kidnapping in 1897. The birthplace given in his passport had to be based on his own sworn statement. Hawaii had been annexed by the United States in 1898 but Chinese born in the islands even before that date had the privilege of American citizenship. If he claimed Hawaiian birth he could avoid the Exclusion Act without pretending to be Japanese. Early in March before he sailed he swore to that birth and United States officials granted him a passport. He seemed to have forgotten that he was a marked man because of other earlier events.

When the *Korea* docked on April 6, he was ready to disembark, looking quite debonair in a Western suit and fedora hat, when newspapermen rushed aboard. The Immigration Department of the United States government was waiting for him. A front-page story including a picture ran in the next issue of *The San Francisco Examiner* under the headline "Manchu's Foe." It said that he used different names, that he once claimed to be Japanese, that many of his own countrymen denounced him.

But what the Immigration Department did was much worse. They hustled him to their detention shed and held him there for three weeks. While he was helpless the papers ran stories about him which made it clear that he had falsified his birthplace in order to get a passport.

None of this really bothered him. What did trouble him was his certainty that the reform group had plotted this detention, and he was afraid they were getting stronger and stronger. He discovered that they were determined to check his influence especially at this time because of an unusual event that was soon to take place. A few days after the *Korea* docked, a Manchu prince was arriving to represent China at the St. Louis Exposition. The United States government was carefully making arrangements to have him met and escorted appropriately. Wealthy Chinese merchants in San Francisco were going to great lengths to welcome him. Neither the United States government nor the local Chinese wanted anything to happen to him, so they certainly could not take any chances with a revolutionist.

Three weeks of imprisonment only made Dr. Sun more determined to do what he came to do. As soon as the Prince had moved on, far enough away to be entirely safe from Dr. Sun, missionary friends posted a bond of $5,000 for Dr. Sun and he was free. By now it was April 26. In spite of the feeling against him in the city, he spoke in public at the Washington Street Theater, and he must have spoken powerfully because the Chinese Consul-General in San Francisco put out a warning against him which was posted all over Chinatown.

The world tour had certainly begun dramatically enough, but now it slowed into a grinding, uphill job. Sun Yat-sen found that the idea of reform rather than revolution had already won over the most wealthy and powerful Chinese in America. He had to turn to the shopkeepers, the laundrymen, the gardeners and laborers for a following. Once in a while he was able to speak to a large group but most of the time he had to talk with a few people gathered in obscure places. When he arrived in a town he looked up possible friends who might offer him a bed, and if that did not work out, he took a room in some cheap hotel. From there he went out to search for any Chinese he could find, his theme always the same, that the Manchu government had to be overthrown and a republic established.

Since Dr. Sun was a church member he could always approach Chinese pastors and hope that he would have a chance to speak to their congregations. Christians usually understood what he said about needing to change China better than non-Christians did because they had been touched by Western ideas and religion. The greatest help of all came from secret societies. On this tour he discovered one called Patriotic Rising which had been started by Taiping Rebellion refugees in San Francisco. It was strong and had branches all over the United States, wherever there were colonies of Chinese, but by now many of the branches had almost forgotten their original purpose and had changed into brotherhoods or guilds which simply helped each other.

Dr. Sun was looking for any help he could get, and he appealed to Patriotic Rising groups wherever they were to be found, sometimes even under a different name, and reminded them of their beginnings. Everywhere he went he found that the idea of reform rather than revolution had to be fought. Even Americans were affected by it. This was hard to understand, for had not the American Revolution been the first of the colonial revolutions? Determined to combat this idea of reform, he wrote a small pamphlet in English, called *The True Solution of the Chinese Question,* and somehow had it published. Its last sentence is, "China is now on the eve of a great national movement, for just a spark of light would set the whole political forest on fire to drive out the Tartar [Manchu] from our land. Our task is great but it will not be an impossible one."[1]

Weeks and months in America stretched into a year. Dr. Sun talked and persuaded his way across the states to New York. There he went to the home of Pastor Huie, who was at the head of a Chinese Christian mission in Chinatown. The pastor and his American wife had met Dr. Sun in the western part of the country and invited him to visit them. Here the revolutionary leader found real understanding. He talked with his hosts, with a number of Christian college students and with others who dropped in to see him. Many young Chinese were now coming to the United States and Europe financed by the indemnity the Chinese government had to pay the United States in settlement of the Boxer Rebellion, which the United States now used in this way.

When the people in Chinatown found out what was going on, they threatened to boycott the mission, but the pastor paid no attention to them.

While Dr. Sun was in New York, his old friend Dr. Hager from Hong Kong attended one of the meetings he led. Dr. Hager and Pastor Huie remarked to each other that while Dr. Sun sometimes looked exhausted and weak, the moment he began to talk about his cause, he lit up and held his audience enthralled. Dr. Sun really liked a small group of listeners best, for then he could just think aloud, aware all the time of the way people were reacting to him.

Dr. Sun had come across Abraham Lincoln in his reading many times, but during these months spent in America the ideas of this great American stood out far ahead of those of other leaders in his thinking. Dr. Sun had been attracted to the "liberty, equality and fraternity" slogan of the French Revolution. He had read a great deal of material by Russian leaders, too, but now Abraham Lincoln's words, "government of the people, by the people, for the people," rang in his mind. Dr. Sun was concerned about people rather than government and he did not think in political terms. As he had crossed the United States, he had touched ordinary folks more than anyone else, ordinary Chinese people. How could he put Lincoln's ideas into words his people would understand against their own background? How could he make them really grasp what he was trying to start? It was much more than an overthrow of government caused by a political revolution. It had to be a grassroots development that would change the way people lived and worked and thought.

Words that seemed right came to him gradually. As nearly as they can be put into English, they were, "The

people are to have, the people are to control, the people are
to enjoy." But they had to be in sloganlike phrases so that
they could be remembered easily. He wrote them in Chinese
characters a number of different ways and tried them out
on his friends. At last the basis of his platform was ready.
He called it simply Three Principles of the People or in
Chinese, *San Min Chu I*. These four words were his slogan
and they soon became the foundation of his party and then
of his revolution, which was now the National Revolution.

Finding a slogan for a party was fairly easy, but this did
not make the party into a strong organization. In the spring
of 1905, Dr. Sun continued his journey around the world,
preaching his theories and searching out supporters for
them. The Manchu government was now providing scholarships for students who went abroad under its new reform
program. By this time quite a group was living in Brussels
because living was cheaper in Belgium than in some other
European countries and they could manage to get along on
their small grants. These students were eager to get acquainted with Dr. Sun and hear what he had to say; they
scraped together any funds they could find and invited him
to come.

This was Dr. Sun's first opportunity to try out his Three
Principles of the People on a student audience. There were
only thirty students there, but that was more than he had
managed to collect in one place anywhere in America.
They were eager and responsive and he was encouraged.
From Brussels Dr. Sun went on to Paris and then to Berlin,
finding a small number of students in each and organizing
them into branches of his Revive China Society.

Although these students were using grants from the Manchu government, they wanted to become members of a revolutionary society. Two of the students in Paris who signed the Revive China Society register were frightened when a third one told them that if Peking found out what they had done, they would lose their scholarships and perhaps their lives. One night they stole the society's rollbook which included their names from Dr. Sun's room in panic, took it to the Chinese Minister, confessed what they had done and begged him to help them with their problem. This man was anxious to avoid any publicity like that that had been connected with Dr. Sun's being kidnapped in London, and he was also secretly interested in the revolution. Now he simply scolded them for stealing the register rather than for joining the society and told them to take the book back before Dr. Sun notified the police, and to beg his pardon. Dr. Sun was not at all upset by all this and did not hesitate to forgive them. The incident was only a sign, it seemed to him, of the warm support the students wanted to give him.

He traveled on eastward, anxious to get back to the Far East as soon as he could, for a whole war had been fought since he left. Japan had declared war on Russia during the winter of 1904 when he was still in Hawaii. The small island kingdom which China had historically looked down on as uncivilized, except as it had learned from China, had been victorious over a great nation of the West. Treaties connected with that victory, which Dr. Sun was interested in, were being drawn up at this time. He went by way of Singapore, stopping to set up branches of the society in wealthy Chinese colonies in the Straits Settlements, then

British possessions. It was pleasant to be an honored visitor in lavish homes. He played his part, dressing jauntily so that his appearance was as modern as his ideas. By the summer of 1905 he was back in Japan.

8. Ten Tries to Make a Dream Come True

Sun Yat-sen arrived in Japan to find that more students than ever were leaving China to study abroad. Japan's victory over Russia had made young Chinese admire her as a modern nation and one who could defeat a white race. As many as 10,000 Chinese students were pouring into Japan to study there within the year, and the rate was likely to continue. A few weeks after he arrived and went to Yokahama, hundreds of them came to meet him, and took him, cheering, to the city's largest hotel where he was to speak. The overflow audience flooded the streets outside the building. Yet, when the meeting was over, he discovered that a good proportion of the young people were reformists rather than revolutionaries, for they had not reacted to what he said with any enthusiasm after the noisy welcome they had given him.

In spite of this, his own plans to overthrow the Chinese government only grew clearer and stronger. Two men who joined him now also influenced him in this direction. They

were Huang Hsing and Sung Chiao-jen, who had attempted
to bring off a revolution in the Chinese province, Hunan,
before Dr. Sun returned to Japan.

In September 1905, after the Russian-Japanese war had
been settled by the Treaty of Portsmouth, a treaty which
was greatly to Japan's advantage and China's loss, Dr. Sun
and his two new helpers called a patriotic meeting of the
students in Tokyo. It was held in the headquarters of the
Twentieth Century Chinese Society. Dr. Sun first made a
speech and then the young men who had come organized
themselves into a new body. It was the Chinese Revolutionary Alliance, but to escape criticism it was more commonly
called the Brotherhood, or Tung Meng Hui. This name was
especially appropriate because members took an oath on
joining just as secret societies required them to do. The oath
said:

> I swear under Heaven that I will do my utmost to work
> for the overthrow of the Manchu dynasty, the establish-
> ment of the Republic and the solution of the agrarian
> question on the basis of the equitable redistribution of
> the land. I solemnly undertake to be faithful to these
> principles. If ever I betray my trust I am willing to submit
> to the severest penalties imaginable.[1]

The new brotherhood came to be known all over the
world by its Chinese name. It had replaced the old Revive
China Society. The Tung Meng Hui was strongly revolu-
tionary and radically socialistic. Its four slogans were:
Drive away the Tartars, Recover China for the Chinese,
Establish a Republic, and Equalize Land Ownership.

Sun Yat-sen was elected to be president of the new

brotherhood, and his friend Huang Hsing became vice-president. Now the doctor was excited and encouraged. He opened a central office in Tokyo and began to dream of completing the revolution in his lifetime. He had more and more reason to have such a dream, for within the next year the membership of the Tung Meng Hui grew to 10,000 and every province in China had its branch. There were also branches in other countries. It pleased Dr. Sun to see that people of all classes were joining the movement. The Tung Meng Hui began to publish its own paper, *Min Pao* or *People's Paper*. Two of the editors were young men who were going to play important parts in China's history in the future. They were Hu Han-min, and Wang Ching-wei, whom Dr. Sun had met at Pastor Huie's in New York. The new periodical was well written and this helped to draw educated people to the revolutionary movement.

Enthusiasm for the revolution began to grow so rapidly that it could scarcely be kept under control. Dr. Sun's magnetism continued to attract young people to his cause. They declared that they wanted to work for it and that they were ready to die for it. A rebellion started by some of the enthusiasts broke out in Hunan Province when it had not been authorized, but young men came to the Tokyo office begging to be sent there to help. Some went without being sent and died there, but the rebellion failed. This sporadic outbreak in Hunan showed how important it was to have a better organization, so it was decided to put final authority in the hands of a small executive committee.

Dr. Sun spent the first part of 1906 traveling to collect funds and at the same time planning a third attempt at the revolution. The first had taken place in Canton in 1895, the second in Waichow in 1900. This time it would again be tried in Canton, in the *yamen*.

It is hard to find out just what happened when the revolution was undertaken this third time but there are indirect reports of it. One comes from an American judge, Paul Linebarger, who was then living in the Philippine Islands and who learned something of it firsthand through his Chinese cook. The cook asked for leave early in 1906 and was gone all summer. When he returned he was badly crippled and the judge found out that he had been summoned to help in the revolution. The judge was impressed by his servant's dedication to Dr. Sun. He seemed to be so devoted to the leader and his cause that the American had a new impression of the whole situation in China.

Another report of this third attempted revolution comes from a member of the Tung Meng Hui whom Dr. Sun had summoned from Hawaii to the headquarters in Tokyo earlier. When this man later went on to Canton, he was astonished to find the doctor deeply involved in managing the strategy there even though he was officially exiled from his country and had a price on his head. The Tung Meng Hui member slept in the room with Dr. Sun and acted as his aide until the Chinese government got wind of the Canton plot. They then escaped to the river bank and managed to hire a boat that was rowed by women. In midstream they persuaded two of the women to sell them their work clothes, which the men put on; so disguised they succeeded in getting away without being recognized.

Again Dr. Sun set out on a tour to raise money and took his cause to Manila, where he met Judge Linebarger whose servant he had called to help him before. The judge was in Tokyo later that year on his way to America. He heard that

Dr. Sun had been asked to give a series of lectures to students in the city but that he had refused, which had caused a great deal of disappointment. He finally found that Dr. Sun had had good reasons for refusing. He had given a speech about his Three Principles of the People to an audience of 5,000 on January 16, 1902, the anniversary of the founding of his paper, *Min Pao*. This event had attracted the attention of the Chinese government and it had persuaded the Japanese government by a series of notes to banish Dr. Sun. Japan had now asked him to leave the country. He did so, taking his two helpers, Hu Han-min and Wang Ching-wei, with him.

The third attempt to bring off the revolution was soon only history but Dr. Sun immediately planned a fourth. It was the largest and the most audacious he had ever thought of. He would invade China from the French border, counting on French help he believed he could get. He would prepare for the dramatic step in the French territories along the southern and southeastern boundaries of China with Hanoi as his headquarters. Dr. Sun worked at top speed, engaging French military experts to train an army, ordering arms and ammunition through members of the Tung Meng Hui in Japan, and calling on young leaders for new devotion. Huang Hsing, who had led the first Hunan uprising, met the challenge by organizing a special group, the Dare-to-Dies, who were soon the core of the rebel forces.

An unexpected development helped Dr. Sun in his new attempt. When the people who lived between Annam and the Chinese province of Kwangsi rose up in a revolt against the taxes they had to pay and the Manchu Chinese government sent forces in to suppress it, Dr. Sun acted quickly to make use of this small rebellion. His propagandists

worked among the rebels and even in the armies that had
been sent against them, to support the protest and win others to the revolution. It seemed to be the moment to avail
himself of a ready-made occasion to launch his invasion.
Once the arms and ammunition arrived from Japan, he
would be able to direct the operations on Chinese soil even
though he had to stay in French territory. He had a total of
8,000 troops and he felt sure that they could quite easily
occupy the two nearest provinces and then move northward
to join armies in the Yangtze Valley which had had some
training in modern warfare by this time. He believed that
they were ready to accept revolutionist leaders. It was a big,
exciting dream, but the arms and ammunition never arrived. Someone had given away the scheme. The military
leaders who had been on the verge of deciding to join Dr.
Sun decided against him now. The revolutionary forces
pushed ahead on their own and won some small victories,
but the imperial troops turned on them and defeated them.
Things were worse than ever, for now the Chinese Manchu
government got in touch with the French authorities and
had Dr. Sun banished from French-held territories. Dr. Sun
left things in the hands of Huang Hsing and went to British-
held Singapore. Huang Hsing carried on bravely and made
four more revolutionary attempts along the border of
Annam before he gave up, at least for a while. A total of
eight tries at the revolution had been made by 1908 and
though a great deal of money had been raised and spent
and although many had lost their lives, all had failed.

Now a new personality came into the long drama of the
revolution. This was an Australian newspaperman named
William Henry Donald. He had reached China in 1903 and
taken up a post in Hong Kong. From there he sometimes

went to Canton when he discovered that that city was a place where young Chinese gathered to talk revolution and to prepare their propaganda. Missionaries told him that some of the young revolutionists in a village near Canton had been caught and executed.

Donald was an unusual person, an individualist, who did not attach himself to the group of other correspondents living in Hong Kong, or join their club and live separated from the Chinese people, as they did. He was soon very much interested in the revolution because he believed that the Manchu government of China was thoroughly corrupt.

In 1908 Donald told the group of revolutionists in Hong Kong that he wanted to join them. This astonished them very much even though they had heard that he condemned the present government of their country. The main reason for their astonishment was that he was editor of Hong Kong's leading English newspaper and also an adviser to the government in Canton. The young men wondered what Dr. Sun would have said had he been there. Sun's helper, Hu Han-min, welcomed Donald, for the Australian was known among Chinese leaders as being thoroughly honest and absolutely reliable in keeping confidences. More than that, everyone had heard that he was fiercely loyal to the Chinese people and determined to do everything he could to help them without thinking of any danger to himself.

In the meantime Dr. Sun, who was now, in 1909, an exile from his own country and had been banished from Japan and from Annam and other French-held territories as well, started on yet another trip around the world to raise money and win support for the revolution. When he was on his way to San Francisco in January 1910, he heard that a new effort to seize the *yamen* in Canton had failed. It seemed that it had come off sooner than intended and that its leader had been killed. Dr. Sun turned back at once and reached Penang, Malaya, near Singapore, in disguise. A meeting of the Tung Meng Hui members in Penang's Chinatown was called to discuss what could be done. Some of those who had been involved in the recent affair in Canton were at the meeting, and when Dr. Sun looked around the group and saw them he realized as he had not before how desperate the outlook for the revolution was at this moment. The society now had almost no funds; many of its members actually needed food and clothing. Their paper *Min Pao* had been suspended by the Japanese government after his banishment. There seemed to be no channel to use for an appeal. But the Chinese merchants of Penang came to the rescue of the situation. They contributed heavily to the cause of the revolution and before Dr. Sun started out again on his world tour, he was able to send between $50,000 and $60,000 to Hong Kong for relief and for ammunition. Such support made him feel under more pressure than ever to make the revolution succeed. This must be the moment for the greatest effort of all, the moment when things would break. It was October 1910 and he was nearly forty-four years old.

Huang Hsing led the tenth attempt at the revolution on the afternoon of the following March 29, 1911. It was once more aimed at the *yamen* in Canton. He himself was at the head of the main column of the attackers while eight other columns made up of about 800 men each were to concentrate on fortifications. Nearly 130 of Huang Hsing's Dare-to-Dies were involved in the attempt, there had for once been enough money, and plans had been carefully laid. But the eight columns did not arrive on time and Huang Hsing and his men were caught alone in the action. The single column fought bravely against 2,000 until at dusk Huang Hsing ordered retreat. By this time 43 of his men had been killed and 29 captured and executed. He had been wounded in the body and had lost two fingers. This incident became known in history as The Seventy-two Martyrs of the Yellow-flower Mound. A monument would mark the spot where the battle took place.

Dr. Sun had been trying to bring off the revolution since 1895. He had used almost every imaginable way of doing it. He had solicited the support of Christians and of missions. He had depended on the strength of secret societies and founded a worldwide one of his own. When he could no longer hide in a British colony, he had made use of Japanese military ability and worked from under the protection of Japan and then of France. He had appealed to the Chinese through his newspaper. Now he quietly resorted to an old Chinese method—terrorism through assassination. When there seemed to be no other way, assassination had for a long time been considered acceptable in China. Now, here and there, Sun's men used it, partly to get rid of someone who was a threat, partly to show the power of his organization.

Ten attempts between 1895 and 1911 had failed to bring about the revolution. Dr. Sun continued doggedly on with his third world tour. He did not realize that a young Chinese military officer, then serving in the Japanese army through an arrangement with Peking, who had joined the Tung Meng Hui after hearing him speak in Japan, was to play a dramatic part in what lay ahead. The young man's name was Chiang Kai-shek.

III. EXIT DYNASTIES; ENTER
THE NATIONALIST GOVERNMENT

9. The Revolution of 1911

The dramatic failure of the tenth attempt to start the revolution in March 1911, and the death of the seventy-two martyrs, whipped up feeling all over China. Those who wanted change helped in laying a new plan for October of the same year.

Perhaps even the people who were working on the new all-out effort for the revolution did not realize how ready the whole country was for it. Several things had been contributing to this readiness. Educated overseas Chinese had supported Dr. Sun's ideals from the first. He had received a great deal of money from them through the years. The merchants of Penang had given strong financial help. The Tung Meng Hui branches had stayed by him loyally in spite of his many defeats.

Other secret societies which formed a network all over China, as well as among Chinese across the world, had spread his propaganda. Some of the best of these societies had come out strongly for the revolution. They specialized in working behind the lines of the imperial army and often succeeded in alienating officers and men in other positions of the government. They influenced the thinking of many Chinese students in Japan, and won them to the dream of a modernized China.

Dr. Sun's newspapers, as well as his articles published elsewhere, appealed to students and intellectual leaders who made up the country's most important class of society. Now they began to take over the leadership in the revolution and were the greatest asset it could have. Small books and pamphlets were printed and added their influence to what the liberal newspapers were already saying. The Three Principles of the People became a slogan that was repeated again and again. A statement of the military purposes of the revolution, called the Manifesto, stirred up feeling and fresh determination.

In Peking things had also prepared the country for the revolution. In spite of Dr. Sun's criticism of it, a program of reform had improved education. Reports were that there were now 57,000 schools enrolling a total of 1,600,000 students, although there were probably 65,000,000 children of school age in the country. A new university, the Imperial University, had opened according to plan. Political changes were being made, too. Steps leading to constitutional government were being taken, with provincial assemblies to be set up first, followed by a national assembly.

All these changes could go forward only if the young Emperor would get behind them; many expected this to happen as soon as the old Empress Dowager died. She had kept him practically a prisoner in the palace in order to check his progressiveness. As things turned out, she was contriving to control events even after she was dead, for when her own death drew near, somehow, his came first. He died a day before she did, and the throne was left to a small child whose father acted as regent and he soon made it clear that he had no interest in reforms. But he could not altogether stop the wheels of change that had already started to turn. The provincial assemblies met in 1909, followed by the first national assembly in 1910. The first parliament with the authority to enact laws was scheduled for 1913. These were steps being taken in the framework of the monarchy.

China was deeply interested in making progress in her methods of transportation, especially in developing railroads. Peking laid out a nationwide plan, and the provinces began to outline their own systems, only to find out that Peking was determined to control all railroads. This discovery stirred up great resentment against the Manchus once more, and when Peking borrowed heavily from foreign countries to start building its railroad systems, there was a loud protest. These loans seemed another form of foreign imperialism and mass meetings were called to denounce the Manchus. Provinces at once suspected, too, that most of the profits would go to the national government rather than to their local governments. Railway Defense Societies sprang up across the country. Feeling on the issue was especially bitter in Szechuan Province because an important line beginning at Hankow would penetrate that section. Railroad riots broke out and these riots unexpectedly connected with the real revolution.

Hankow was chosen as the place where the new revolutionary attempt should be made. This city, located on the Yangtze River at a point about 650 miles west of Shanghai,

together with the nearby Wuchang and Hanyang, made up
what is known as Wuhan. This three-city area was China's
industrial center and had iron works, granaries, coal fields,
and the wharves necessary for shipping and transshipping.
Oceangoing vessels could navigate up the river to this point.
These facts made Wuhan a choice spot for rebellion, for it
was in touch with outside influences and yet on the main
lines of communication to the interior.

Preparations for the revolution went on intensively now.
Revolutionary leaders harangued great meetings, gave out
literature and tried secretly to win over some of the imperial
troops stationed there. When the riots over the railroads
broke out in Szechuan Province, two regiments of the imperial troops were dispatched from Wuchang to put them
down. The revolutionists decided that it would be to their
advantage to act while these forces were away. New dates
for the attempt were discussed, but whether one was decided upon is not clear, for an accident brought on the
revolution.

Dr. Sun was back in the United States by this time, trying to raise more money, after the heartwarming incident in
Penang when the merchants contributed so generously.
Word of the Chinese Revolution was everywhere now and
many people were sympathetic toward Dr. Sun's efforts and
failures. One evening after a meeting a small hunchbacked
man named Homer Lea came up and offered himself to the
revolution. He had once been to China, had written a book
on military strategy, and considered himself an expert on
the subject. He had once been a strong supporter of the
reformists, but now he wanted to help Dr. Sun. The doctor
was touched by his offer and promised on the spot to make
him his military adviser if he was ever in a position to do so.

This kind of quick reaction to friendly help was characteristic of the Chinese leader, but Homer Lea was both astonished and delighted.

The exact itinerary of this tour is not clear from the records but it included not only the United States but Canada, London and other points in Europe. In Canada Dr. Sun met up with another young man who wanted to devote himself to the revolution by becoming one of a bodyguard, which Dr. Sun now submitted to having at least part of the time. It would have been hard to find two people as unlike as this young Jewish man, Morris Cohen, and Dr. Sun. Cohen was unschooled, effusive and without any serious ambition except to make a fortune and experience adventure. He had gone to Canada from England when he was sixteen and fallen in with a Chinese *tong* or secret society. He had learned of Dr. Sun and the revolution through one of the men in this society, and through him also discovered that Dr. Sun was coming to Canada. Cohen had heard so much about the revolution from the Chinese that he was greatly excited when the moment of being introduced to Dr. Sun arrived. The young man wrote about the experience later and said that he had never before in his life met a really great man but that he had instantly recognized Dr. Sun as one. His complete devotion to the Chinese leader began at that time and did not end until Dr. Sun's death.

Dr. Sun proceeded across Canada, accompanied by Cohen and two Chinese who were also part of the bodyguard. After the two-month tour was over, Dr. Sun commissioned Cohen to secure arms for the revolution, a responsibility which Cohen accepted joyfully. He had become an ardent supporter of the Chinese cause, making speeches wherever he could and soon even drilling a small company of men whom he dreamed of somehow getting to China. After Dr. Sun left for Europe and then the Far East, Cohen kept in touch with events as well as he could although the two men did not see each other again until 1922. This long interval was partly because of Cohen's part in World War I.

While Dr. Sun was still somewhere in the United States, moving eastward, he received a cablegram from Hankow. It was sent in a numerical code because it was too difficult to use characters in telegrams, and his codebook was with his baggage, which had gone ahead to Denver. Two weeks later when he caught up with it he deciphered the message and found that it was from the revolutionists, asking him to send them some funds as quickly as possible. They were ready to start the revolution

To give him time to think over what to do he decided to wait a day before replying to the message. The next morning, reading a newspaper while he was eating breakfast in a restaurant, he was shocked by a glaring headline: "Wuchang Occupied by Revolutionists." What had happened? What ought he to do? Why had the revolution been updated? He was careful to give no sign of his anxious excitement because any unusual behavior might draw attention to him and give away his identity. Newspapermen would then soon pick him out and begin to question him. He ate his meal as though nothing had happened. After fifteen years of devoting his life to the cause, after ten tries and failures, the revolution was on!

If he started for Shanghai he could make it in three weeks, but they would need more money than he had yet been able to raise. He knew he was no military leader; he could be more useful by continuing his fund-raising. Setting out for New York, he stopped off in St. Louis. There he saw a paper which said that the revolution had begun on his orders, that a republic was being established and that he was to be its first president. He shrank from the idea of holding such an office. Through the years he had been trying only to free China from the reign of a corrupt foreign dynasty and establish a new democratic government that would put her in her rightful place in the modern world. He had no personal ambitions.

Now he concentrated on trying to build up friendship and support for his country. America was already friendly to her new ideas, and France was friendly, too. Germany and Russia would not be able to understand the real significance of what was happening in China, but surely England would. He set out for London to see what support he could get there from the British government, carefully remaining as inconspicuous as possible and giving no indication of his identity. His Chinese friends protected him from any publicity as much as they could.

When he reached London Dr. and Mrs. Cantlie again took him in, although they were half afraid that the Chinese legation would give them trouble. In spite of all they had been able to do to maintain secrecy, a steady stream of messages to them had announced Dr. Sun's coming. Dr. Sun himself was astonished to find a warm welcome among the British people. Their Sunday newspapers applauded the Wuchang uprising. He had to make sure of three important things: that Britain would keep Japan from interfering in Chinese affairs, for England had just renewed an alliance with Japan; that his earlier deportation papers from England were cancelled; that Great Britain would help the new republic with loans in connection with a new plan for international financial help called the Reorganization Loan, as well as with diplomacy. He talked with the proper authorities and felt that he had succeeded on all three points. When the necessary papers had been signed, he went to Paris and looked up Americans in authority there to get the same assurances he had secured in England. Again he was successful.

At last he was ready to start home, and he no longer needed to pretend he was anyone except Dr. Sun Yat-sen, founder of the Chinese Revolution. He had been hanging around little laundries in Chinatowns, acting like a nondescript Oriental, half afraid that he would be discovered and get all the wrong kind of publicity and even have a new price put on his head. All that was over. He made himself known and newspapers around the world quickly acclaimed him as the one who was bringing a new day in China. They called him the leader of the Chinese Revolution, the founder of the republic, the new president of China. He was forty-five, his hair gray, his large eyes still deep and soft, his mouth so gentle it could be called weak. Even under anxious conditions he had always managed to appear calm, but now at last he could *be* calm as well. On November 11, he sailed for Singapore and China, content. Another passenger aboard the ship and also bound for China was Homer Lea, the military strategist.

The revolution, which had been planned for so carefully this time, had come in this way. On the ninth of October, 1911, a rainy day when twilight was just falling, some of the revolutionaries gathered in an upper-floor room of an old mansion in the Russian concession in Hankow. In the basement hired technicians had a bomb factory where they were preparing for the next attempt at the revolution. While the small group upstairs discussed things quietly, calculating when everything would be ready and wondering where Dr. Sun was by this time, the building shuddered from a terrific explosion. Windows across the street were shattered. The revolutionaries managed to escape to Wuchang by boat, but on their way they found that the book containing the list of local members of the Tung Meng Hui had been left behind. Although it was dangerous evidence, they could not risk going back for it.

A German butcher not far from the explosion was closing up for the night when he heard the roar and felt the earth shake. He called the police. The viceroy of Wuchang immediately seized the roster and the documents left by the revolutionaries, as well as all the ammunition, and arrested more than thirty of the listed people. The government artillery and the engineering corps had secretly been won over to the revolution, and when eight of them were executed for stealing guns, the entire group mutinied and attacked the viceroy's *yamen*, burning it to the ground. The viceroy escaped with some of his officers, leaving the armies behind in complete confusion. When he managed to board a gunboat near a British warship in the river, he sent a message to the British consul saying, that the outbreak of hostilities was antiforeign, hoping so to enlist the help of some foreign nations. None were willing to be involved in what was happening.

The city of Wuchang was in the hands of the rebels by October 11. Another of the triple cities, Hanyang, with its steel works and arsenal, and Hankow, the third, both fell on that same day. On October 12, the provincial assembly of Hupeh Province, where Hankow stood, convened and declared itself independent of the Peking government, call-

ing on all the other provincial governments to do the same.
But the revolutionaries had to have a leader since Dr. Sun
was not there. Huang Hsing was on his way, coming as
quickly as he could, but they did not know this, and they
went to find a man who had been with the imperial armies
but had come over to their side. This officer, Colonel Li
Yuan-hung, was far from eager to take command. When
they finally located him, he was trying to hide. He did not
agree to serve until one of the men held a pistol to his own
head and threatened to commit suicide unless he agreed.
The revolutionaries wanted more than his reluctant word,
so they produced a statement calling on the whole country
to unite against the Manchus and demanded that he sign it.
He was an unenthusiastic leader for so dramatic and signifi-
cant a movement as was now sweeping China, but at least
he could serve as a figurehead.

All this had taken place with enormous speed while the
chief dreamer and originator was still far away. Perhaps
because he had not been in China during the bloody events
of the revolution's beginning, he seemed to have no connection with them when he did arrive. He was the hero, his
hands clean and his gray head ready for the laurel wreath of
honor.

Macao, China. The pioneer city of European trade with the Orient.

The new house built for the family by Sun Mei.

Sun Yat-sen at eighteen.

Sun Yat-sen standing between two other young revolutionaries in 1895.

Huang Hsing, leader of the Dare-to-Dies.

View from the wharf, Hong Kong, China.

The Tomb of the Seventy-two Heroes,
Temple Hill, Canton, China.

Dr. Sun Yat-sen and his bride, Soong Ching-ling.

Dr. Sun at home at 29 Rue Molière, Shanghai.

Burdened and ill.

Dr. Sun Yat-sen's will with signature.

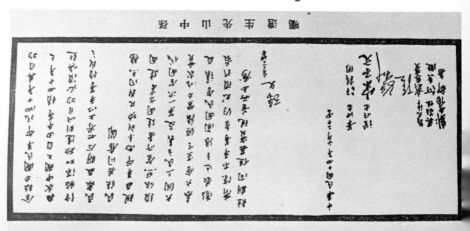

10. A Victorious Leader

When Dr. Sun's ship reached Singapore on December 24, 1911, a great crowd was waiting to welcome him and a wealthy Chinese friend pushed his way through to take his hand and lead him to his house. Going on to Hong Kong, Dr. Sun landed almost without remembering that sixteen years before he had been denied the right of setting foot there. In Shanghai a deputation boarded his ship to accompany him ashore and proudly posed for pictures with him. The press wanted a dramatic statement from the new republic's founder and leader. When he overheard someone in the crowd say that he had collected enormous sums of money, he announced loudly and clearly, "What I bring back is not money, but the revolutionary spirit."[1]

Soon he found that things had been happening too rapidly in China for him to realize them. He struggled to catch up with events. On the fourteenth of December Huang Hsing, who had arrived while Hankow and Hangyang were being taken over by the revolutionaries, had been appointed acting president with Li Yuan-hung still president. At that very moment the northern forces had met those of the south; that is, the government forces moving down from Peking had confronted the revolutionaries. Shanghai had been taken for the revolution and the young military leader, Chiang Kai-shek, had been called from Japan to help and had seized the *yamen* in the city of Hangchow, which was not far from the great port.

Dr. Sun soon discovered that things were in a state of confusion in Peking. Some generals had taken a stand for a constitutional government and had approved the assemblies. Others had not. Sabotage had grown so serious that the government had made a military man named Yuan Shih-kai premier, in order to check it. He had acted without hesitation to dismiss the regent and introduce a new constitution, and then at the head of his own armies had gone to join the imperial forces. When he was near enough the revolutionaries to do so, he had sent emissaries suggesting a mutual peace with Britain's foreign representatives to act as intermediaries. Now Li Yuan-hung, the half-hearted president of the republic, had had to face Yuan Shih-kai, a clever militarist, in the negotiation. During the peace talks, Nanking had fallen to the revolutionary forces. One of the imperial army commanders had changed his allegiance and helped the invaders. Nanking's fall was highly important because the city controlled the Yangtze River Valley and all that lay southward.

Dr. Sun arrived in Shanghai at this moment and was encouraged to find that the peace conference between north and south seemed to be moving along well with an armistice in effect. Some questions were still being discussed in

Peking, but a national council made up of representatives from all the provinces that had declared their independence was called to meet on December 29, a few days after he landed. All the desperate failures of the past seemed to be fading away and now, at last, the Manchu government was tottering. Surely China was ready for a new role in the world, Dr. Sun told himself.

The doctor had always had a mild, almost humble, bearing except when he was making a speech. But these days, under the glow of good news and the pleasure of being welcomed as a hero, he radiated unusual happiness while he was in Shanghai with old friends. On New Year's Day, 1912, he boarded a train for Nanking. That very afternoon he was elected to the office of provisional president of the republic of China by a specially called council, which was in session. He took the oath of office in proper Western style, promising unity of the various peoples of China, devotion to their common cause, protection of foreigners in the land, and other good measures. Much of what he said was based on his Three Principles of the People. At midnight the booming of guns, celebrating his inauguration, shook the city. Writing of many events that had led up to this great moment in his autobiography sometime after this, Dr. Sun said, "On that day I saw the successful accomplishment of the great ambition for which I had struggled during thirty years, the restoration of China, and the establishment of a republic."[2] The autobiography does not mention the fact that one of the people who saw the glorious moment of inauguration was the small, frail Homer Lea, whose dream of becoming the president's military adviser now seemed to come true. That dream failed, in part at least, because Lea was already an ill man. He was returned to the United States within a few months and died before the first year of the republic had passed.

As the voice of New China Dr. Sun had to make a public statement to the world. He telephoned the republic's office in Shanghai for help and the men there asked the Australian journalist W. H. Donald to work out something suitable. He sat down at his typewriter in an unheated room and tapped out what he thought was right, glad to have the chance to do something for China. His draft was discussed, added to, subtracted from and rewritten a couple of times before everyone was satisfied. It had to be just right. The final statement was privately called the "Donald Manifesto." On January 25 governments around the world read the first official statement of the new republic. President Sun Yat-sen, without a change, had signed what had at last been produced.

The peace talks that had been going on had not unified China. Peking was still the capital of a monarchy in the north, while Nanking was the capital of a republic in the south. In the north the child Emperor chosen by the Empress Dowager was still on his throne. Yuan Shih-kai, the military man who had been made premier, had sent representatives to the peace talks but he was angry because Dr. Sun had been elevated to provisional president before the peace talks had been finished. Now everything pointed to an outbreak of war, rather than peace, and southern armies began to move quietly northward.

Chinese leaders of the republic asked each other desperately what could be done to save the new-born democracy. There were anxious conferences and hopeless suggestions. One thing they did not dream of was that their leader would act without consulting them, but this was what he did. He simply telegraphed Premier Yuan Shih-kai and offered him the office of president, on certain conditions. The conditions were that the Emperor abdicate, that there be a complete break with the Manchus, and that the republic be fully accepted as the form of government.

Even Yuan Shih-kai seemed to think such steps ought to be made in a more orderly way, and he suggested calling a meeting of the national assembly. He knew that it would take some time to convene, and he wanted to delay any great change. Government funds were low, whether for empire or republic, and he knew that Dr. Sun was trying to negotiate a loan from Japan using the Hanyang iron works as security.

Perhaps Dr. Sun did not know that Japan was also offering the Manchus in the north military assistance until W. K. Donald discovered it. The Australian quickly prepared a dispatch demanding that Japan announce a public repudiation of any help being given the Manchu government. China's Minister in Tokyo, who was to present the dispatch to the Japanese government, was afraid that such a repudiation would bring on war with Japan but Donald, acting for Dr. Sun, fought through all arguments. A copy of the dispatch went to the British Minister in Tokyo because Britain had a pact with Japan and could influence that country's international actions. A few days after the statement had reached the British Minister's hands, a report from Tokyo stated that Japan had decided to stay neutral in the Chinese situation. Two days after that a London dispatch reported the same policy on the part of the British government. W. K. Donald had played it hard for the country he had by now adopted as his own.

Something had to crystallize soon out of the uncertainty that hung over the divided country. The generals of the imperial army helped by presenting a statement to Premier Yuan Shih-kai saying that they urged the adoption of the republic because their troops were no longer to be counted on. They were not being paid. Yuan Shih-kai accepted the statement as an easy way to make the change and slip into the leadership himself. He had edicts drawn up announcing the institution of a provisional republic because "the majority of the people are in favor of a republic."[3] Dr. Sun argued that the republic could not be set up as a continuation of the Manchu dynasty. Yuan Shih-kai said that that was not what was in mind. His statement satisfied Dr. Sun and he announced his intention to resign from the office of provisional president of the republic of China, after filling the position for two weeks. The same special called council that had elected him now elected Yuan Shih-kai in his place. In many ways it was a relief to Dr. Sun. He was a dreamer, a reformer, but not a political leader. He was inexperienced in governing a country. Yuan Shih-kai, on the other hand, had commanded armies for many years and he had been premier. Surely, Dr. Sun thought, it was a good arrangement; Yuan Shih-kai had been properly rewarded for getting rid of the Manchu dynasty, and the republic had a good leader.

China was making such a dramatic break with her past that there had to be some celebration. The day after Yuan Shih-kai became president the whole government group (Yuan himself was delayed in Peking) made a pilgrimage to the famous Ming dynasty tombs on Purple Mountain, near Nanking. The founder of that dynasty had lived in the fourteenth century, and now Sun Yat-sen reported what had happened to him, in the ancient traditional manner. For centuries events had been recounted to the spirits of those already gone, at the site of their tombs. On this occasion the retiring provisional president, his cabinet, his civil and military officers, as well as the modern army units, were present in formal array.

When Europeans and Britishers and Americans read about the ceremony at Purple Mountain, they were astonished. Here was an antiquated rite mingling in with a modernized China's transformation in the oddest way. It seemed so out of keeping with all they had been hearing about the republic. But the young Chinese did not think it strange. They were used to this reporting to the dead, both in the family and on more formal nationwide bases. It was also an event at which great pomp and power and dignity could be displayed, and the new government needed this kind of public display.

There were other formalities to be carried out. The new president was to be inaugurated in Nanking, which was to become the new national capital. President Yuan Shih-kai seemed to be making his plans to be there at the proper time, but one event after another delayed his coming. When the date was postponed time after time, he at last suggested that the inauguration be held in Peking rather than Nanking to simplify things. This was reluctantly agreed to. On that same day the national council in Nanking adopted a provisional constitution and Dr. Sun and his cabinet resigned. This meant that he had given over all of his powers to Yuan Shih-kai, a former military leader of the Manchus. Also, the fact that Peking, the Manchu capital, had now become the temporary capital of the new republic, made some feel that not very much had been changed by the revolution. But this was not the way Dr. Sun felt. He seemed to be thoroughly satisfied with developments, and he gave no sign of not having complete faith in the new president.

Dr. Sun Yat-sen was China's most popular figure, a symbol of a new day. He was welcomed and feasted and photographed wherever he went. He was asked to speak and he spoke with all his heart and all his burning magnetism for the republic of China, which he had devoted his life to creating.

11. An Honored Guest
at Home and Abroad

Sun Mei, Dr. Sun's brother, had retired and had in 1909 moved from Hawaii to Kowloon near Hong Kong, bringing their mother and Dr. Sun's wife and their two daughters with him. Sun Fo, the son, was grown by now and had entered the University of California. When the revolution began he had hurried to China to see his father elected to the presidency and to try to help his country. Mrs. Sun Yat-sen had come to Nanking for the great celebrations connected with the inauguration. When these special events were over, Sun Fo returned to college in the United States, taking his sisters with him.

Now that Dr. Sun was no longer president, he made more public speeches than ever. Perhaps he was secretly glad to be relieved of the political responsibility the highest office would have put upon him. Certainly he had not lost any of his old ability to charm his audiences. His voice was almost a monotone when he began to speak then it took on the curious quality that made those who listened sit for-

ward in their seats so as not to miss a word. He described
the steps that he thought China had to take in order to build
a good and a secure government and these were based on
his Three Principles of the People. Some Westerners who
listened to him thought that his ideas were quite socialistic.

In the summer of 1912, President Yuan Shih-kai invited
Sun Yat-sen and General Huang Hsing to Peking, but
Huang was suspicious when he discovered that two important revolutionists who had been visiting the city had just
been executed, and he refused to go. He tried to dissuade
Dr. Sun from accepting the invitation, too, but Dr. Sun
was curious to see what was happening in Peking and he
planned to go. There seemed to be factions in the new national assembly, which had now taken the place of the national council. Part of the cabinet had even resigned. In
spite of this an important event took place on August 13.
The Tung Meng Hui joined with some other smaller groups
to form the Kuomintang or National People's Party, usually
called the Nationalist Party. Two weeks after its formation
it met officially for the first time, in Peking, just a few days
before Dr. Sun arrived there. This new organization was
much milder than the earlier Revive China Society had
been, and less revolutionary than the Tung Meng Hui. It
said that its objectives were to bring the people a better
standard of living and to develop the resources of the country through a socialistic government.

When Dr. Sun reached Peking at the end of August, he
was given royal treatment. The mother of the child Emperor sent him polite messages. One of the princes, as her
representative, gave a great feast in Dr. Sun's honor. This
was the very prince whose trip to the United States years

before had caused the American immigration officers to detain Dr. Sun in San Francisco for three weeks. If anyone thought of it, he gave no sign.

Dr. Sun made speech after speech. He even addressed a great audience of Christians, some of whom came great distances to hear him. Dr. Sun told them that his dream of revolution and a new China had originated with his contact with missionaries. Now, he declared, the republic would fail unless it was righteous.

President Yuan Shih-kai and Dr. Sun spent many hours conferring together, Dr. Sun explaining his theories and his programs and his hopes. There was no argument between them, for Dr. Sun had a good impression of the old-fashioned Yuan, especially since he said that he agreed with all that was being proposed.

One of Dr. Sun's dreams was of a great network of railroads spreading across the country. He had presented the President with a ten-year scheme that would include building 75,000 miles of government-owned lines costing $3,000,000,000 in Chinese money. The President approved the plan and appointed Dr. Sun to head the country's railroad development and asked him to provide specific blueprints, get estimates from foreign engineers and financiers, and then apply for the government's approval. Dr. Sun was to have $30,000 in Chinese money a month as a working fund, but he would have to depend on foreign loans for the building of the railroad system.

Railroad lines had been laid across some parts of northern China at a rather fast rate in the ten years before this, and Dr. Sun now made many trips to see them before he started south. A party went with him on his observation

tours. This party included Mrs. Sun and his secretary, who
was Charlie Soong's oldest daughter, Ai-ling. Wang Ching-
wei and W. K. Donald, the Australian, were also in the
group. Wherever the special train on which Dr. Sun was
traveling stopped, even at small country stations, bugles announced its arrival and crowds of people were there to welcome him.

Donald had time to talk with Dr. Sun and to try to understand him. They discussed the plans for the railroad system and began to visualize a map. Early one morning Donald was summoned to Dr. Sun's car to look at a map which
the Chinese leader had already drawn up as a rough basis
for their work. Many years later Donald remembered that
morning and his first view of that map. Dr. Sun had not paid
any attention to mountains or rivers or other natural obsta-
cles but had simply laid down the proposed lines as a small
child might do it. Donald glanced at him quickly, expecting
that his face would break into a joking smile, but Dr. Sun
was perfectly serious. What a horrible situation, Donald
thought to himself. Somehow he must protect the leader
from criticism. If experienced people ever saw that map,
Dr. Sun would instantly be disqualified from carrying out
the plans he dreamed of. Donald borrowed the map "for
study" as soon as he could in order to keep it out of the
hands of pressmen who crowded aboard the train when it
drew into the station of a large city. Dr. Sun must be protected legally, too. He must have authorized rights to get
the contracts for the railroads. Donald drew up a charter
which gave the doctor legal power to negotiate the program, and had it properly signed. The Australian drew a
deep breath of relief. What a dreamer Dr. Sun was! His feet
never seemed to touch the real earth. Yet it was his undying

dream that had materialized in the revolution. He was a giant in promoting renewal and change, but a mere child in carrying them out, Donald decided. Someone was simply going to have to protect him from his own innocence. When the tour was over, Dr. Sun opened his railroad construction office in Shanghai with his map prominently displayed. Let it hang there, Donald thought. It was like an embryo, like the first faltering blueprint of any grand design. Other maps would follow it.

There were old faces in the new office. Charlie Soong acted as treasurer, and he was efficient. Charlie Soong's daughter, Ai-ling, acted as secretary as she had on the tour, and she was precise. Wang Ching-wei was another indispensable member of the railroad office staff.

Once the railroad program seemed to be in motion, Dr. Sun went to Japan in February 1913, taking Mrs. Sun and Ai-ling with him. They were provided with a private coach on the Japanese Imperial Railways, and when they drew into Tokyo 3,000 Chinese students gave Dr. Sun a wildly enthusiastic welcome, throwing flowers and presenting scrolls of congratulation. He and his little party were feted and honored at every turn. Perhaps Dr. Sun had expected this kind of a welcome in Japan; certainly there were good reasons for it. He had escaped to Japan in 1895 after his first attempt at revolution when he had cut off his queue and put on foreign dress. He had remained in Japan most of the time between 1899 and 1903. He had returned there again in 1905 after his second tour around the world, although he had not been able to stay because the Chinese Manchu government had made it impossible for Japan to give him refuge any longer. The Japanese people had helped his movement by giving it money and arms and experts. He had often slipped across the narrow sea to the islands, secretly, because liberal Japanese leaders welcomed him to their homes and shared whatever they had. The Japanese had given him the name Nakayama, or Chung-san in Chinese, which means "central mountain." This name was to become popular in China, too, in later years.

Against all this background, the great welcome by the Japanese people was not surprising, but when the welcoming was over, they waited to see why he had come this time. Was he a representative of President Yuan Shih-kai? Had he come to thank Japan for past help? Was he sent to promote commercial interests between the two countries? Was there hope of new ties between the altered government of China and that of Japan? Had Dr. Sun come to get loans for his railroad program?

Answers to some of these questions were not hard to find. Dr. Sun could not be an official representative of the Chinese republic because that government had not yet been recognized by foreign powers. It seemed most unlikely that Dr. Sun was in Japan to build political ties between the two countries because Yuan Shih-kai had been suspicious of Japan's interest in China for a long time and had even fought her policies in Korea. Now it made him cringe when he read of all the friendly gestures being made to the Director of Railways in Japan.

It did not take long to find out that Dr. Sun had come to Japan to get loans for China's railroad program. During the short time that he was provisional president of China he had mortgaged Hanyang's ironworks to Japan for loans. The Japanese now began to suspect that he had other such steps in mind, and yet that was hard to believe, too. Would he not realize the danger of letting Japan get control of

China's important industries? While he appeared disarmingly innocent, he might not be innocent at all.

Back in Peking President Yuan Shih-kai was at the same moment working on the tremendous plan for the vast foreign loan called the Reorganization Loan. Several nations were to be approached for funds and Japan was one of them. The loan was intended to stop foreign nations from competing for concessions from China by getting international loans set up in place of loans from individual interested nations. This was the plan Dr. Sun had known of when he was in Great Britain on his way home, securing the promise of that country not to loan money to the empire that was still in power then, but to the republic that was just in creation.

For all the welcome and ceremony, Dr. Sun failed to get railroad loans in Japan now in 1913. What he heard about steps being taken in Peking in regard to the Reorganization Loan made him furiously angry. The loan body said that it had to have a sound security and that it would be satisfied with China's national salt tax if it were administered by foreign customs offices or some other foreign service. Such conditions were highly embarrassing to the young republic. Surely Peking would not accept them, Dr. Sun thought, but it did. Even then the whole plan moved only very slowly along. Some funds were advanced by the Reorganization Loan, but even with the humiliating conditions, money did not come quickly. Foreign powers that were involved held back, waiting for China's government to settle down and get organized. They were suspicious of the stability of the republic. They were suspicious of President Yuan. They tightened their conditions more and more, and because of the desperate financial situation, President Yuan tried to meet them. China used various ways of raising funds at home, but the sums that could be gotten were too small to meet the crisis.

At this crucial moment the United States withdrew entirely from the Reorganization Loan body. President Wilson said that his country felt such a plan invaded China's independence. Chinese who had opposed the loan suddenly felt very proud of China's sovereignty although that sovereignty was more shaky than ever because one of the six nations in the Loan, and an important one, had abandoned it.

The United States withdrew at the very time when Dr. Sun was leaving Japan to go to Peking and report on his trip to Yuan Shih-kai. He did not have any idea how badly things had gone at home during the few weeks he had been away. While he was still at sea, a murder brought on disaster. A man named Sung Chiao-jen had been assassinated.

IV. THE STRUGGLE TO SAVE A VANISHING DREAM

12. The Second Revolution and Romance to Soften Its Failure

Sung Chiao-jen had gone to see Dr. Sun in Tokyo with Huang Hsing in 1905 and had played an important part in founding the Tung Meng Hui, becoming one of its strongest leaders. He was also one of the editors of the *Min Pao*, or *People's Paper*, and an able spokesman for the revolutionary cause. Later, he took a leading role in forming the Kuomintang or National People's Party on the foundation of the Tung Meng Hui, and had a hand in writing the provisional constitution for the republic.

On the night of March 20, 1913, while Dr. Sun was returning to China, Sung was about to board a train in Shanghai and was standing on the platform talking to Huang Hsing when a shot rang out. The crowd scattered and Sung fell dead, killed instantly by an assassin's bullet. Huang Hsing quickly remembered the two murders of the year before when he had refused to go to Peking with Dr. Sun. He was positive that President Yuan had maneuvered those and now this one. Sung had been too open in promot-

ing parliamentary reforms and opposing the Reorganization
Loans, just too strong and outright a leader, Huang Hsing
thought sadly.

When Dr. Sun's ship reached Shanghai five days after the
murder, he was surprised by the emotion of the tremendous
welcome the crowds gave him. He was even more astonished when police from the International Settlement closed
in around him, for he did not know that the Kuomintang
papers were openly charging the leaders in Peking with
Sung's murder. Even less did he suspect the full significance
the assassination was going to have for him. Swallowed up
in the crowd and then surrounded by police, he suddenly
understood that the Chinese people were turning to him as
their only hope. That was why they were giving him such a
welcome. They believed that only he could save the republic, for they were being betrayed by President Yuan Shih-
kai.

This was the kind of challenge that Dr. Sun rose to meet
with zest. He immediately drafted a nationwide call for a
new revolution to overthrow Yuan Shih-kai, for in his heart
he already knew that the republic was failing. He had secretly despaired of Yuan Shih-kai's ability to lead a new
government. Dr. Sun wanted to send out the call for revolt
at once, but Huang Hsing begged him to wait; after all, the
republic had been established legally and it would not be
wise to ask for illegal action yet. At his urging, Dr. Sun
agreed to a delay.

The national assembly met in April but soon fell into
disagreement, first over the election of a speaker and then
over the Reorganization Loan. The President announced
that the loan had already been approved by the legislature

and could not be discussed again. By early May Dr. Sun was so upset about the loan that he privately sent a cable to his friend Dr. Cantlie in London, denouncing it as having been settled unconstitutionally and begging Dr. Cantlie to get Britain to intervene against it from that end. The cable did no good; Dr. Cantlie, of course, was not in a political position to do anything.

China's situation grew steadily worse. Her leadership was divided. Yuan Shih-kai and the old favorites of the Manchu regime who were supporting his government were on one side. The modernists were on the other. The republic tottered toward collapse.

The summer of 1913 was disturbed by uprisings in many parts of the country. Li Yuan-hung, once the unwilling provisional president, was now the viceroy of Wuchang. He severely repressed a rebellion that started there in June. President Yuan replaced three Kuomintang provincial governors with his own men, bringing on more outbursts. The moment to declare the Second Revolution had come. Now Dr. Sun sent out a public telegram that demanded President Yuan's resignation, but Yuan paid no attention to it. On July 12, rebels attacked the government garrison in Kiukiang, a Yangtze River port. Two days later Nanking declared its independence under the leadership of Huang Hsing while four whole provinces joined the revolt at once. There was fighting in Shanghai. Chiang Kai-shek was about to leave for Germany to study military tactics when the local revolutionary leader, Chen Chi-mei, summoned him to help in an effort to capture the arsenal outside the city. The attack failed but they did succeed in taking control of the telegraph system. Although the fighting went on for almost ten days, the revolutionary forces finally had to withdraw because the government bombarded them with its gunboats.

The Second Revolution was over almost before it had begun. On July 23, Dr. Sun was removed from his position of Director of Railroads, and by August 8, newspaper headlines announced that he was on his way to Japan. His route was actually very indirect. Escaping from Shanghai on a German cargo boat heading for Canton, he hoped to help carry out a revolt that was being planned there, but the ship stopped so long at ports on her way that by the time he reached Hong Kong he found that everything was already over in Canton. Another attempt had failed. Dr. Sun went on to Formosa and then to Tokyo. On October 10, 1913, Yuan Shih-kai was inaugurated President. Foreign powers took part in the ceremonies recognizing the republic.

Tokyo soon became a gathering place for the leaders of the revolution. They came to be known as the Revolutionary Committee. The Soong family was in Tokyo and Charlie Soong, was still serving as treasurer. Ai-ling, his oldest daughter, who had been Dr. Sun's secretary a few months earlier, was now married, but her younger sister, Ching-ling, who was just back from college in America, took her place. She helped eagerly, glamorizing the revolution and its leader. The youngest of the Soong sisters, Mayling, was still studying in the United States.

Dr. Sun's own family was having problems, although he scarcely took time to notice them. When Mrs. Sun was in Japan the last time, at the moment when he was receiving so many ovations, she had faithfully tried to play her part but the publicity had been hard for her to bear. When she and Dr. Sun returned to China their older daughter came home to them from America, ill. This time when Dr. Sun went to Japan, Mrs. Sun did not go with him. Instead she took the sick daughter to Macao and nursed her until her death later the same year.

Soong Ching-ling, Dr. Sun's new secretary, had become very much excited over what was happening in China when news of the revolution reached her in America. She dreamed of the country as practically remade and imagined Dr. Sun as a great and triumphant leader. While she was still in college her father sent her the five-barred flag of the Chinese republic and she tore the old dragon flag of the empire from the wall of her dormitory room where she had hung it, and stamped upon it. She loved English literature courses and one day wrote a glowing essay about her country for the college magazine, in which she said, "For centuries the Chinese have been a peace-loving people. They have esteemed the arts of peace, and neglected the arts of war, worshipped the scholar and slighted the soldier. China, with its multitudinous population, and its love of peace—love in the real essence of the word—shall stand forth as the incarnation of Peace. . . ."[1]

Working as Dr. Sun's secretary in Tokyo, Soong Chingling did not look like a girl who would write such impassioned words. She was beautiful in a delicate sort of way and restrained in her manner, but she felt things deeply. The failure of the revolution had disappointed her keenly and personally. She could not fail to see how Dr. Sun smarted under the disappointment. She threw herself into helping him in as many ways as she could, and there were many. She could write and speak both English and French fluently, she was modern in her way of thinking, she was young and enthusiastic. She believed in the revolution, and she believed in Dr. Sun Yat-sen. Although he was forty-eight, she grew to adore him.

During those months spent in Tokyo Dr. Sun attempted to hide himself from publicity, wearing Japanese clothes and living with Japanese friends. But he was in constant touch with the Revolutionary Committee. Sometimes General Chiang Kai-shek came there and Dr. Sun began to see possibilities in using him for military work, but he was not ready for any great new steps. He was discouraged and even bitter. He thought over the past as he read the news of what was happening in China and sank into deepening despair. President Yuan Shih-kai was determined to get rid of the Kuomintang. He first expelled all members of the party from the national assembly, and then he openly dissolved it. These drastic steps forced Dr. Sun to a sweeping decision. He would start a new party here in Japan, for the Kuomintang had lost all its revolutionary zeal and become politically soft. It had abandoned its original purpose, which was to overthrow oppressive governments.

No one knows how much he talked this idea over with other members of the Revolutionary Committee in Tokyo, but on July 8, 1914, he established the Ke-ming-tang, or Revolutionary Party. He was to be its head and all its officers were to be responsible only to him. Everyone who became a member would have to take an oath of loyalty to him personally and pledge it with his fingerprint as his seal. Some of his old friends objected so strongly to the oath and the fingerprint that they quietly disappeared, not wanting to disrupt his plans with argument, for they agreed that a new party was needed. Two who left were Wang Ching-wei, who went to France, and Huang Hsing, who went to the United States.

This time Dr. Sun did not go abroad to solicit help from overseas Chinese. Instead, he depended almost entirely on Japanese. He seemed to feel that Japan as a neighbor and a strong, partly modernized nation would be the deciding factor in whether he succeeded or failed. "If Japan helps me, victory will be on my side: if she helps Yuan Shih-kai, he will conquer," he declared.[2]

All that really lifted the gloom for him during this dark time was Soong Ching-ling's steady enthusiasm and reassurance. She came into his life like sunshine and in spite of himself he was warmed and cheered. They could not keep from falling in love with each other. Divorce was still very unusual in China in the early 1900s. It was much more usual for a man to take a second wife, who had a recognized place in his home, if he wanted to. But even this was usually done when the first wife failed to have a son to carry on the family name. Mrs. Sun had not failed in any such way, however. Dr. Sun had still another problem when he fell in love with Ching-ling: he and the Soong family were both Christian. Christian society would permit divorce. Chinese society would not. Mrs. Sun, who was not Christian, was willing for Dr. Sun to take a second wife, but she would not let him divorce her. There seemed to be no solution. Somehow, quietly, in Japan, a kind of divorce or separation was arranged which would not remove Mrs. Sun from her position. On October 25, 1914, Dr. Sun Yat-sen and Soong Ching-ling were married in Japan. They were criticized by both Christian missionaries and non-Christian friends, but as time passed the criticism died down. The young Mrs. Sun was accepted, for the couple were clearly devoted to each other. Ching-ling threw herself into working with the Revolutionary Committee in Japan and in serving as an able and imaginative secretary to the man she more than ever thought of as the founder of the republic of China.

13. Who Will Help?

Dr. Sun stayed in Japan from 1913 to 1916, a period during which the First World War broke out. These three years in Dr. Sun's life are ones which historians argue over because the records of what he was doing are not clear. We know that in his discouragement at what had happened in China he attempted the Second Revolution, and that when that, too, failed, he turned to Japan for help. It seems certain that he must have gone far in making promises to Japan that would give her rights to develop China's railroads and commercial economy, and also permit her to supervise her interests in China, in return for her military help and leadership in overthrowing the Peking government. Dr. Sun was risking more than he realized; in his eagerness to succeed in bringing off the change to which he had devoted his life, he seemed blind to Japan's real intentions. He did not seem to see what history has proved true, that Japan at this time had in mind a scheme to take over control of her great neighbor. A Japanese secret society called the Black Dragon Society was hard at work on such a plot, but Dr. Sun evidently did not read its statements. These would surely have raised his suspicions, for they declared that the society was planning uprisings throughout China that would overthrow the Peking regime and allow their men to take over the country.

Although China remained neutral until nearly the end of the First World War, this did not keep her from being affected by it. German rights in the coastal city of Tsingtao in northern China had been secured in 1898 under a ninety-nine-year lease, and Germany had built a great naval base there. The agreement stated that her rights could not be transferred to any other foreign country. Now, because of the war against Germany, British and Japanese forces seized the base, but England was so deeply engaged in Europe that she left it to the Japanese to manage. Japan also took over the German railroad in the province of Shantung where Tsingtao stood. The Chinese government tried to get Tsingtao back by declaring the city out of bounds in the war, but the Japanese press quickly denounced China for this effort. What came to be known as "The Shantung Question" was soon the center of an international argument with many side effects.

On January 18, 1915, the Japanese Foreign Minister in Peking did an unusual thing. He went to the presidential palace and presented a diplomatic note in person, even though this was properly done through a country's minister of foreign affairs. The fact that the usual courtesies were not carried out was in itself an affront to China, but the contents of the note went far beyond disrespect. It contained demands which asked China to give Japan permanent controls in Tsingtao and in Shantung Province, concessions in Manchuria, mining and railroad rights in the Yangtze Valley, and to employ Japanese advisers in many important positions of the Chinese government. It also stipulated that no other foreign countries were to be given the same privileges, so that Japan would really be in control of a large part of China's future. When word of the Twenty-One Demands leaked out, reaction to them was furious.

President Yuan Shih-kai had been suspicious of Japan for many years. Though he now kept up a conciliatory front toward Japanese officials, he was strongly opposed to the demands. Still he was enough of a politician to realize that in the end China would have to work out some sort of a compromise with Japan instead of rejecting what she asked outright. The situation grew more urgent as leaders among the reformists attacked President Yuan Shih-kai, as well as Japan, through the press, and students all over the country rose up in loud protests.

Yuan Shih-kai was now the central figure in a terribly dangerous and difficult situation. He fought off the Japanese proposals gamely although he was truly in an impossible position. Since he had been made president, he had had to try to use the methods he had used in military and monarchical settings to carry forward the democratic forms of a republic, and this could not be done successfully. The two objectives and systems could not be combined. When Yuan Shih-kai had realized the dilemma he was in, as he soon had, he had secretly begun to plan to swing back to monarchy and had resisted going forward toward democracy any more than he had to. He quietly waited for the moment to come when he would be able to reinstate the empire.

While all this was going on in China, Dr. Sun was still in

Japan. When the Twenty-One Demands were proposed, people began to suspect that his interest in getting Japanese help may have involved him in playing a part in them. Then news of what he had actually offered in return for Japan's commitment to help him leaked out. Secret memoranda, threats and alleged statements bearing his name, whether they were authentic or not, were circulated. It still seems hard to believe that he never suspected Japan's dream of aggression in China. Historians ask themselves whether he could have been so hopeful and trusting, or whether he felt he had to take such desperate risks in order to drive his bargain with Japan. Perhaps he would have been more anxious about Japan's intentions if Huang Hsing had been with him, but Huang Hsing was still in the United States.

Dr. Sun had reason to be depressed over the political state of the republic, for Yuan Shih-kai was gradually dropping the marks of a democratic government as he had decided to do. He had abolished presidential elections; his office was now for life. He had replaced Kuomintang men in high positions with his own personal friends. He had revived many of the old practices of the empire and was again carrying out public ceremonies connected with the form of government he liked best. He had also improved his own personal army, since he was still a warlord, so as to be ready for any future events. When the Twenty-One Demands were first presented to him, he had even momentarily considered opposing them by military force and then had realized that it would be a foolish step for him to take. His forces were not equipped to meet the power of modern Japan; besides her own army, she was allied with the great military countries of the West, all of those at war against Germany.

For five months President Yuan Shih-kai tried to resist the demands, and then he attempted to tone them down. Japan finally set May 7 as the deadline for settlement on her terms or war. President Yuan had no choice but to accept the basic requirements presented him. Reaction to this decision was swift and strong. The revolutionaries blamed President Yuan personally. They instigated outbreaks all over the country in protest. Chen Chi-mei, the revolutionary leader in Shanghai, was determined to resist Japan's taking over the industrial developments in the Yangtze Valley, and he was not going to let go of Shanghai. He had the city's defense commissioner assassinated and then attacked the government cruiser *Shao Ho* and won its allegiance to the revolution. He used the ship to bombard the Shanghai arsenal and while that was going on he and Chiang Kai-shek, who was in Shanghai at the time still delayed from his trip to Germany, attempted to get control of an important Shanghai suburb. But the *Shao Ho* had to withdraw under the heavy counterfire of other warships on the river, and the revolt failed.

A strange thing now developed in Peking. President Yuan Shih-kai had an American adviser named Professor Frank Goodnow, who was an expert on writing constitutions. He drew up a plan of government for China that would give the office of president great power, which was exactly what President Yuan wanted. Yuan moved quickly to put the American adviser's ideas into action since it was obvious to him that a monarchy would be better for China than a republican form of government. He engaged the help of a monarchical secret society in whipping up public opinion to support his plans, and it published a pamphlet called *Constitutional Monarchy, the Salvation of China.* It at-

tacked the revolutionaries, especially Dr. Sun. Thousands
of copies of this little book were scattered over the countryside. On January 1, 1916, Peking announced a new government, a new dynasty with Yuan Shih-kai its emperor.

Dr. Sun, still in Japan, protested, but his protest was mild
compared with that of the reformer Liang Chi-chao. This
man had tried to help Yuan Shih-kai resist the Twenty-One
Demands, but he was by no means ready to support Yuan
as an emperor or to agree to an empire. Liang went to the
far-off province of Yunnan, secured the help of a general,
and organized a revolt. Yunnan Province declared its independence of Peking, and six other provinces soon joined it
in what was called the Third Revolution. It was clear that
although the republic had not been a success, the Chinese
people were far from ready to go back to the old days of
empire again. Public opinion against what Yuan had done
was strong. The intellectual leaders opposed it, too. Besides
this, Yuan soon found that diplomats from other countries
stationed in Peking disagreed with his ideas. He was planning a coronation ceremony for himself but when even his
closest friends advised against it, he decided to abandon the
idea. Thinking that he could still patch things up, he rein-
stated the republic within three months after he had declared himself emperor, but it was a hopeless thing to do. In
another three months he was dead. Some people said that
he had died of a broken heart. He had certainly been humiliated by all that had happened and had floundered desperately in trying to find some acceptable course to follow. All
real power now rested with Vice-President Li Yuan-hung,
once the provisional president of the infant republic, and
later viceroy of the city of Wuchang.

When Huang Hsing, still in the United States, heard of

all that was happening in China, he hurried back to the Far East although he was quite ill. After he reached Shanghai he grew worse and died in a few months' time. Li Yuan-hung continued in power. He had never been a true revolutionist and now he began to strengthen his personal position. He was glad to have Huang Hsing out of his way. He wanted also to get rid of Chen Chi-mei, who had tried to take the Shanghai arsenal and suburbs, for that man showed too much ability and was not safe to have around. Li sent conspirators to Shanghai. Even though Chiang Kai-shek, suspected a plot and warned Chen Chi-mei against them, they assassinated him.

Sometimes the Second Revolution is thought of as a dividing point in Dr. Sun's life. Up until the quick failure of that attempt he had always been full of hope, for he had believed that he was leading his country under a mandate from Heaven and that he would therefore surely succeed. He had counted on help from the western hemisphere. But after the Second Revolution and his humiliation at its failure, he had become bitter and willing to use almost any means to salvage his life's work. Arriving in China in June 1916, after three years away, he stepped into the middle of a melodramatic scene of change and death, but he seemed almost unaware of most of what had happened and was happening. He appeared to be confident and strong.

The war was still going on in Europe, and early the next February President Woodrow Wilson urged all the neutral nations to break off relations with Germany. This included China. The Chinese government at once asked the German and Austrian Foreign Ministers to leave Peking, but she was reluctant to declare war, for declaring war was very complicated. Premier Tuan Chi-jui was in favor of it but parliament, which had just gotten started again after the reestablishment of the republic, wanted to concentrate on working out its constitution. The premier decided to talk things over with leading military men and called them to Peking for a conference. They all favored entering the war and the cabinet agreed. When the question was formally presented to the parliament, a mob gathered outside and demanded that it agree to the step. Premier Tuan Chi-jui was then accused of staging the mob so as to get his way and the cabinet resigned, leaving the premier with only the support of his military men. Parliament and public opinion demanded the resignation of the premier, but he refused to resign and President Li dismissed him. While parliament argued over the constitution, some northern provinces declared their independence. Parliament was dissolved by a military man and its members escaped in disguise. Military power was taking over as the only real authority in the shambles of government.

At this point a reformer slipped into Peking and tried to set things straight by getting the young Emperor brought out of hiding and reenthroned. The show lasted about two weeks and was ended when Premier Tuan Chi-jui took over Peking by military force. This was too much for President Li Yuan-hung to bear. He refused to be president any longer. The vice-president assumed the office and Tuan Chi-jui, who had seized the city, continued as premier.

The country was divided over the issue of whether China should declare war. One half was made up of militarists, who were really out for themselves, wanting to get back what Japan had taken and thinking only of China's military strength. The other half consisted of the revolutionaries, who were trying desperately to get a constitutional government on its feet. The militarists centered in the northern part of the country, the revolutionaries in the southern, although there was no clear-cut division; some patriotic and intelligent men in Peking were hard at work drafting a constitution and were not at all ready to submit to the aims of the militarists.

Dr. Sun fought China's entering the war with all his might. He had settled in a house at 29 Rue Molière in the French Concession in Shanghai and from there he did everything he could think of to stay the decision. He even wrote to Prime Minister Lloyd George in England, charging that English agents were working behind the scenes in China, trying to get her into the war. He also intimated that a great power like Britain ought not to need China as an ally.

But what Dr. Sun was most afraid of was that China's participation in the war would involve her in more disorders and that the weak republic would be destroyed by fighting between Chinese factions. While China's help in the war was mostly in the form of labor battalions made up of conscripted "coolie" soldiers, Dr. Sun watched the growing military spirit in the country with dismay. As long as Yuan Shih-kai was in charge, whether he was president or not, he had been the master military man. Now that he was gone, others were having a free-for-all to get control of Peking.

At last Dr. Sun decided to make one more effort to get order in the capital. He appealed to Premier Tuan Chi-jui, who, after all, seemed progressive in his thinking, either to revive the constitution and make a start toward organization, or to resign so that someone else could. He hoped that the premier would get to work, for he had stood up against Yuan Shih-kai, he had retaken Peking when the child Emperor had been put back on the throne, and now he was premier again under a reestablished republic. But Dr. Sun's appeal failed.

Now Dr. Sun looked southward for help. He collected the revolutionaries in Shanghai around him, commandeered all the fleet he could bring together, and planned to sail to Canton. The revolutionaries in Shanghai still had memories of their great dream. They had suffered for their cause. At this point they abandoned all hope of a constitutional government in Peking. Some of them had fled from that city to take refuge in Shanghai, for they had seen what was going on in the capital firsthand. All joined in the plan to go to Canton and sent out a declaration. It said that any legislative decisions taken in Peking from this moment on would be illegal and that they were going to reconvene the true patriots of the constitution in another place. On a strange, dramatic day they posed with Dr. Sun for photographs before they sailed in a group for Canton on July 17, 1917, accompanied by most of the Chinese navy.

Although this was a tragic moment for China, it was a high moment for Dr. Sun. For three years he had been in hiding in Japan. Since he had returned to Shanghai, he had been almost as obscure, spending most of his time writing in his home in the French Concession. But now he was stepping out again as a leader. He had his faithful followers around him, and Canton was always a good place to plant and tend revolution. Perhaps even yet, the old dream of a new China could come true.

14. Drama at Canton

Dr. Sun wanted to set up the government of the republic in Canton, and to make Canton into a model city. It seemed to be his best hope because three factions, under warlord leaders, were fighting among themselves in the north. He felt sure that his own group in the south would soon demonstrate what it could do. It was a new day for him.

On August 14, 1917, China declared war on Germany and Austria. She had several reasons for taking the step, the most important one being her fear of Japan. Japan already had those rights in Shantung Province and at the Tsingtao harbor. What might she not demand in war settlements? The question of the war settlements was one of the major ones in China's decision to enter the war, for she was determined to be a party to whatever agreements were made.

At first Dr. Sun's plans seemed to go well. He was following the requirements of the 1912 constitution. The parliament that had been dissolved in Peking on June 17 gathered again in August of that year in Canton and two weeks later set up a provisional military government to serve temporarily, electing Dr. Sun its head, or generalissimo. Everyone hoped Li Yuan-hung would come to Canton and assume the presidency. Sun Fo, who had graduated from college, joined his father to help as secretary to the government. The city celebrated its progress. Dr. Sun sent out strong statements to Peking and began to plan expeditions against that city once again. But although outwardly things seemed to be encouraging, Dr. Sun had to play a game of factions in and around Canton. Only four of the six important southern provinces had come out for the new Canton government and these four were controlled by other military leaders who each claimed two. The fifth and sixth provinces each acted independently; thus there were actually four factions, not counting the city. Canton itself was controlled by a military man, or warlord, named Chen Chiungming, making a fifth faction.

These factions did not stay at peace with each other very long. They soon fell into two groups; Kwangtung Province faction (Dr. Sun's), and the Kwangsi Province faction. Dr. Sun's faction found that he was very hard to work with and so they set up a committee, of which he was one, to act for them. Before long he decided that the committee arrangement was unworkable. He admitted that he was defeated by it and, abandoning his great plans for a government in Canton, he returned to Shanghai in May 1918. There he lived quietly until the summer of 1920, while Sun Fo stayed on in Canton as a journalist.

Although Dr. Sun had been devoting his life to the revolution, he seemed to have paid little attention to a great deal of revolutionary activity that had been going on in the country since the death of Yuan Shih-kai in 1915. About that time progressive magazines slanted toward young people began to pour out of the presses, influenced especially by a Chinese professor at the Peking National University. The famous American educator, John Dewey, joined that staff in 1917. In the meantime, Hu Shih, who was later ambassador from his country to the United States, modernized the Chinese written language, with sweeping effect. The written and printed word was now suddenly understandable even to those who had not been educated in the classical forms. The whole change was labeled the Literary Revolution.

The Russian Revolution in October 1917 had excited many of the Chinese people, too, especially the younger ones. They began to ask why their own revolution had failed. They had thought it was patterned after the American and the French, but the results had been disappointing. When he had heard of what was going on in Russia, Dr. Sun had remembered the conversations he had had with the Russians in the library in London. On an impulse he had sent a telegram of congratulation to Lenin in Moscow. That telegram had made Lenin wonder whether his new ideas of government might not be applied in China, too.

At the close of World War I, the terms of peace drawn up at Versailles gave Japan the former German possessions in Shantung Province. China had hoped to get these back after the war; this had been one of her big reasons for entering it. On May 4, 1919, students protesting the decision at Versailles began what became the May Fourth Student Movement by staging strikes, burning the homes of Japanese diplomats and inducing the merchants to carry out a severe boycott of Japanese goods. Labor unions joined in, too, for they were newly organized and conscious of great power.

In July 1919 Russia sent a proposal or manifesto to Peking. It was named the Karakhan Manifesto after the man who framed it. The Chinese government ignored it, but many Chinese intellectuals learned of it and felt that Russia was far more friendly and conciliatory than other foreign powers were. The manifesto declared that all the old Tsarist treaties with China were annulled, that all Russian concessions in China were to be restored to her and that all Russian citizens living in China would from this time on be subject to Chinese courts rather than to their own in the concessions, which had been the practice. Russia also removed her share of the indemnity imposed on China by foreign countries after the Boxer Rebellion and drew up a new treaty for the Chinese Eastern Railway, which cut across Manchuria linking China with Russia. China in return for these things was to cooperate with the new Russian government and establish new trade relations. It was not surprising that some of the more liberal Chinese began to think favorably about what was going on in Russia.

Although all these events were closely related to Dr. Sun's dreams, he had taken no really active part in them nor did he now after abandoning the attempt at government in Canton. He stayed quietly at 29 Rue Molière, spending most of his time writing. When his article, called *China's Revolution*, was finished, those who read it were surprised to find that he had used the old, stilted Chinese forms. It was true that when he lectured he was lively and modern in his style, but his way of writing had not changed in spite of what Hu Shih had done.

Younger leaders, truly worried about their country, were beginning to realize that the great change that Dr. Sun was hoping for was not possible. It was not possible to form a democracy because the people had not been educated for it. One young man who had been with the labor battalions in France had come to see this especially clearly. When James Yen returned to China he decided to attack this situation, and he organized a system called the Thousand Character Movement to teach literacy. He hoped that, through this system, people too old for school could learn to read enough words to understand directions, know what was in the newspapers and be in touch with the world. Perhaps one day they would even be able to help a democracy work. If Dr. Sun knew what Yen was doing or how it might affect his cause, he gave no sign. Perhaps this was because he seemed unable to break free from his personal aim of setting up a revolutionary government within his own lifetime, and that lifetime was shortening.

But Dr. Sun was not able to keep from thinking about Canton as the place where the new government for China must be tried again, not for long. In 1920 he sent word to Chen Chiung-ming, the warlord, to get rid of the rival Kwangsi Province faction in the city, implying that if this could be done, he would throw his support behind Chen once more. Chen relished the assignment. He set out under the slogan "Kwangtung for the Kwangtungese," and succeeded.

Now things were encouraging; Dr. Sun went back to Canton. The Chinese Revolutionary Party which Dr. Sun had organized in Japan became part of the Kuomintang. When parliament reassembled in 1921 it elected him president of the Chinese republic. This meant more to him than others may have realized for, even though only Kwangtung Province was now under his control, he thought of himself as president of all China. He at once set about making this a fact. First he made Chen Chiung-ming governor of the province and commander-in-chief of the troops. Chen's assignment was to win back the allegiance of adjacent Kwangsi Province; it had always been closely related to Kwangtung despite the recent hostile faction. Again, Chen was successful in his undertaking.

Dr. Sun's second step in extending the power of the republic was to make plans for an expedition to Peking, the Great Northern Expedition. Chen did not agree with this idea at all, but it made no difference to Dr. Sun. The President was self-assured and encouraged now, and he declared that if Chen would not lead the expedition, he would do it himself.

In the early autumn of 1921 Dr. Sun set out on this difficult undertaking. Chiang Kai-shek, who was now a general and one of the young military leaders in Canton, was very much upset both at what Dr. Sun was about to do and at the faith he was putting in the warlord Chen. Chiang Kai-shek urged Dr. Sun to give up the idea of leading the expedition, but the older man did not pay any attention to him. Dr. Sun had not gone far with his troops when he began to get reports that Chen was sabotaging him from the rear. Money and supplies intended for the expeditionary forces were not reaching them. Chiang Kai-shek knew that this was happening and, even worse, that Chen's power in Canton was becoming dangerously strong. He believed that Dr. Sun was being betrayed.

Dr. Sun could not and would not turn back now. He pressed on, negotiating for free passage through the next province he had to cross. Then he got word that Chen's chief of staff had been murdered in Canton. What was the meaning of this? He could not get reliable information on anything, it seemed. He became so frustrated because of lack of supplies and wild reports that he at last decided to give up the expedition temporarily and return to Canton.

In Canton in early April of the next year, once again he acted severely. He removed Chen Chiung-ming from his position as governor of Kwangtung Province and commander-in-chief of the troops, leaving him only as Minister of War. It was a dangerous thing for Dr. Sun to do so summarily, for Chen was embarrassed and furious. Chiang Kai-shek could scarcely believe the news. He had never seen a man like Dr. Sun; he must be either fearless or simply unable to see the danger in situations. Chiang was not sure yet whether it was courage or stupidity.

The new governor of Kwangtung Province, a man named Wu Ting-fang, who as Foreign Minister to Washington had finally managed the freeing of the elder Lu imprisoned in Choyhung and was always a loyal supporter of the revolution, advised Chen Chiung-ming to take his troops out of Canton. Chiang Kai-shek had already thought that Chen might try to take over the city, and he urged an attack on this man at once before he had time to act. But Dr. Sun was not ready to listen to anyone's advice. As for this young military man, Chiang, he seemed to be ready to tell everyone what to do. Why was he suddenly so much on hand? Where had he been these last few years? Some people said he had been playing the stock market in Shanghai, and now he seemed to have appointed himself adviser! The president had little patience with him.

Dr. Sun had no intention of giving up the Great North-

ern Expedition. In a few weeks, after he felt that he had
straightened out things in Canton, he set out again. His
troops were fighting their way north through Kiangsi Province, in the Yangtze Valley, when fifty battalions of Chen
Chiung-ming's men cut off his retreat to Canton by a flank-
ing movement, and occupied the city for themselves. Dr.
Sun succeeded in entering Canton again but with only his
bodyguard. Two weeks later a rebellion broke out among
Chen's men, the very ones who had outflanked Dr. Sun's
forces. That night, June 15, 1922, a telephone message
warned Dr. Sun to leave the presidential mansion at once or
risk losing his life. He refused. An hour or so later his
secretary and another member of his staff came by carriage
to beg him to escape. They told him that there were 25,000
troops in the city and they were getting entirely out of control. Dr. Sun still refused to go. He said that it was his duty
to stay by and help stop the rioting, that he would be ridi-
culed if he ran away from the situation. He would not
change his mind, and the two men who had tried to rescue
him left in desperation.

At two o'clock in the morning, they returned because
something had to be done about Dr. Sun's safety. By now
looting had begun, houses belonging to Kuomintang leaders
were in flames, and gunfire could be heard. Under their
extreme pressure Dr. Sun finally agreed to leave. He talked
things over with his wife and they decided that she was to
wait where she was with a bodyguard of fifty men. To avoid
suspicion, only three persons were to accompany Dr. Sun.
By this time sentries were posted all along the way, and
everyone would be challenged. He and his party of two
would have to travel in disguise.

The plan of escape succeeded although at one time the

three men had to pretend to be looters in the Ministry of Finance offices to avoid being noticed. When they reached the naval headquarters on the bank of the Pearl River, Dr. Sun wanted to stay there. The admiral, however, refused to have him because he would not accept responsibility for his life. Dr. Sun and his men then quickly took refuge on a small Chinese navy gunboat, the *Yung Feng,* anchored in the river.

In the meantime the rebels, who had been surrounding the presidential residence since the day before, wondered what was happening. They had been sure that Dr. Sun would try to escape by car, but no motor car had left even by three o'clock in the morning of the sixteenth. They decided to storm the palace, offering $200,000 reward for Dr. Sun's capture and promising a holiday as soon as that was accomplished. Such a holiday would mean letting the soldiers do as they pleased, a thing to make Dr. Sun's friends' blood run cold.

Aboard the gunboat Dr. Sun was still assuming leadership. He gave orders for two cruisers to get upstream to a point where they could bombard the rebel forces. When the cruisers returned the next day after carrying out their assignment, delegations of sailors came aboard the *Yung Feng* to declare their loyalty to Dr. Sun. This touching experience was one part of a day of contrasts: while this was going on, Chen Chiung-ming publicly demanded Dr. Sun's resignation. Instead, Dr. Sun decided that he would order the troops then on the expedition north to come home and put down the rebellion in Canton.

A time followed when no one could find out what was going on. Dr. Sun did not even know what had happened to Mrs. Sun. He needed someone he could rely on to help in a

number of ways and suddenly thought of Chiang Kai-shek.
Now was a chance for that young man of many ideas to
show what he could do. The only trouble was that Chiang's
mother had died and he had gone to the home village for
the usual period of mourning.

Dr. Sun had seven warships under his command while
Chen Chiung-ming had three. Chen was rumored to have
gotten these by bribing them to come over to his side.
Whether this was true or not, they managed to take an
important military base at a place called White Goose Pool.
Dr. Sun ordered the *Yung Feng* to approach and open fire
on the base. His ship was struck six times, but the attack
was indecisive. The fighting went on in a halfhearted way
week after week, and the summer came on with increasing
heat. On July 19 some kind of a torpedo hit the *Yung Feng,*
but Dr. Sun, who was eating lunch at the time, did not pay
much attention to it. The other men in the cabin hurried
around muttering against Chen and suggesting all sorts of
things that ought to be done until Dr. Sun said mildly, "He's
only trying to frighten us into a truce." He lifted his cup of
tea and drained it before he looked at any of them.

Chen Chiung-ming was doing exactly what Dr. Sun had
said, but Dr. Sun had no intention of such a settlement. He
was not going to give up. Instead, he dug in for a period of
watching and waiting. An American newspaperman came
aboard the *Yung Feng* and asked Dr. Sun for a statement.
". . . If I preferred life in these circumstances to death, how
could I face the revolutionary martyrs and the youth with
equanimity? I am determined to fulfill the early ambitions
which I have cherished for thirty years, and if necessary I
shall die for the republic," he said.[1] Dr. Sun now sent a
message to Chiang Kai-shek by telegraph, begging him to

come in such dramatic terms that Chiang wondered what could possibly be happening to make Dr. Sun beg *him* to do anything! News was scarce and what came through was so unlikely that he had not paid much attention to it. His old home village, set among picturesque mountains, was beautiful and peaceful.

Dr. Sun waited for news of the Northern Expedition, which he had decided not to recall after all, to see what progress it was making, and waited for General Chiang. Things seemed to be settling into a pattern for the time being. Then someone used the clever trick of starting a rumor that the president-in-exile had died. Dr. Sun was amazed to see how powerful such a rumor was. Was he *that* important, even now when he was unable to leave his little ship? When word of his supposed death reached the expeditionary forces they were temporarily demoralized, and lost an important town. Fate seemed to be against them. They had been cut off in the rear, their supply columns had not worked properly from the start, and now rumor shook their determination.

When Chiang Kai-shek arrived, hurrying as quickly as he could, he found Dr. Sun outwardly calm, but beneath the calm he showed strain. Dr. Sun immediately made him chief-of-staff, an office which under the circumstances meant anything. Sometimes he swept the decks to keep the crew from complaining and threatening to mutiny. Often he disguised himself and went ashore to buy food, especially something that would appeal to the poor appetite of the President. Chiang had a rare chance to study the older man and try to understand him. He saw that while Dr. Sun was naïve and unrealistic, he had great idealism and vast courage. It was not so much that he did not foresee failure as that he paid no attention to the possibility. Dr. Sun, too, lost some of his opposition to the younger man. They lived together on the little ship for fifty-six long, hot days.

Chiang Kai-shek discovered that Mrs. Sun had not reached the *Yung Feng* for several days after her husband took refuge there. She had had a terrifying escape. The presidential palace stood on a hillside and the rebels had stationed themselves above it. From there they had kept up a steady stream of fire all night after Dr. Sun had escaped. At last Mrs. Sun, a foreign adviser and two guards had decided they would have to make an effort to get away. They crawled along a bridge passage that connected the presidential residence with the offices. Just a few minutes after they left, the palace was attacked and the guards killed. Now the little group of escapees dared not go forward and they could not go back. They waited in agonizing anxiety hour after hour and then at last crept on to the government offices. The dawn had passed into morning and then afternoon. Now a mob roared at the government offices. They had only one chance: to lose their identity by joining the mob. As part of that raging mob they saw how terrible the state of Canton was. Warships on the river had been shelling the city and had set it afire. Dead bodies were strewn everywhere. The little party once or twice fell to the ground and pretended death to escape questioning. Getting up when the moment had passed and pushing on again, they had at last reached a farmhouse on the outskirts of the city. There, Mrs. Sun had fainted. When they could they had gone on again for two more days before they had reached the *Yung Feng*.

Chiang Kai-shek heard her story and looked at the couple. How different they were from each other! Yet he saw that they openly adored each other. He had met Mrs. Sun's older sister, Ai-ling, but he had not yet seen the younger, May-ling, although he knew that she had returned to Shanghai after finishing her education in America. What would she be like, he wondered.

Now he felt a new pathos in Dr. Sun's situation. He was already fifty-five years old, Wu Ting-fang, his good friend, had died during the terrible days, his faithful bodyguard had been killed, and he had lost all his precious books and manuscripts. The city of Canton, which he had loved all his life and wanted to make into a model city for the new China, was burned and in ruins. The realization of his dreams seemed farther away than ever, for there was no use in pretending that he was not defeated. He had to leave Canton and the only way that he could do it safely was by getting the help of a neutral nation. The British consul at Canton arranged for Dr. Sun and a small party to be transferred to a British gunboat and from there to a liner sailing to Shanghai. When they docked on August 15, 1922, Dr. Sun made a public statement to the world, declaring that he had been betrayed but that he would never give up the struggle for the Kuomintang.

Once more he was in the French Concession in Shanghai. Once more he had to think things through and lay plans. Chiang Kai-shek saw that although the leader was bitterly disappointed, he did not intend to accept failure.

15. Dr. Sun and the Communists

While he was still in Canton in 1921, Dr. Sun had met some Russian Communist agents who had come to look things over and report back to Moscow. One of them was a Dutchman using the name Maring, who discussed what was taking place in Russia and pointed out the progress that had been made in both the political and economic situations. Dr. Sun was greatly impressed by what he said. Maring suggested that the Chinese Revolution could be helped in two ways; by making use of the structure of the Kuomintang to help itself politically, and by building up its military strength possibly through the assistance of the Soviet Union. Dr. Sun asked himself whether it was not possible to set up some kind of an alliance between Germany, Russia and China to help his own cause, but he kept the question to himself. Maring went to Shanghai and in June of that same year he helped to organize a small Chinese Communist Party, which a number of Chinese leaders took part in. One of them was the professor at Peking National University who had been editing a progressive magazine; another was a man named Mao Tse-tung.

After Dr. Sun left Canton because of the rebellion there, Maring came to see him in Shanghai and talked with him again about the role of the Kuomintang. Then the new Soviet envoy to Peking, Adolf Joffe, wrote to Dr. Sun discussing the relationship of the new Communist Party to the Kuomintang. Dr. Sun believed that it would be all right for the Communists to join the Kuomintang as individuals but not as representatives of their Party. He felt that the two groups ought to be entirely separate as organizations. Long before this time he had tried to explain the goals of the revolution in his Three Principles of the People. Although unexpected events had forced him to adapt and change his methods, his goals had not been altered. They were still to free China from foreign powers and Chinese warlords, to carry forward a political program that would pass through a stage of chosen political bodies instead of inherited monarchy or military dictatorship, to true democracy "of the people, by the people, and for the people." Dr. Sun was not willing to have Communist Party influence change these goals.

Adolf Joffe proposed a formal Sino-Soviet relationship while he was in Peking but he failed in getting this through. In December 1922 he went to Shanghai and met Dr. Sun there. Joffe had been educated in the United States and was a man of great personal charm. It was hard to resist him. He treated Dr. Sun as if he were still president. After long talks together they came to an agreement in January 1923. The agreement was very much like what had been proposed in the Karakhan Manifesto. Its significance for China was that she was to be treated in terms of equality with a foreign power. This decision had the effect of making Dr. Sun feel more favorable than ever toward Russia although he did not really understand what was happening in that country. He did not have the right background to comprehend it. He had been drawn to European-Christian culture when he was still very young, and he had seen these demonstrated through Christian missions and through his travels in America and Western Europe. They and his Chinese classical education made up his preparation. But he was sure that the Russian people were making dramatic progress and that was what he wanted for China. He asked himself how he could best lead on now, isolated as he was in Shanghai while Chen Chiung-ming still threatened every effort in Canton.

Colonel Morris A. Cohen, who had helped to procure guns and had been assigned to guard Dr. Sun when he was making a Canadian tour years ago, came to Shanghai in August 1922. Dr. Sun had written to him to ask him to collect information on railway construction and bring it to Shanghai, for Dr. Sun had still not given up his dreams of developing a national rail system. Cohen had accepted the assignment joyfully because he was still a faithful supporter of the Chinese leader and wanted to join his revolution, even if he could do no more than continue to be his bodyguard.

Arriving in Shanghai, Cohen excitedly asked his way to Dr. Sun's house. When he reached 29 Rue Molière in the French Concession, which continued to be the only home the Chinese leader owned, he found a small, unimposing building, instead of the rather grand residence he had expected. The room where he was received was decorated with only one picture, that of Abraham Lincoln. When the doctor came in, Cohen thought how little he had changed. His moustache was gray and his hair thinner at the temples but his figure had not altered. Though he did not laugh easily, his eyes often twinkled. Cohn noticed that he still did not smoke and that he drank only tea or fruit juice. Though nearly a dozen years had passed, everything was as it had been. When Dr. Sun asked Cohen to be one of his three aides-de-camp, the Canadian accepted the charge enthusiastically. As a member of his staff, Cohen lived in Dr. Sun's house. It afforded a chance to become really well acquainted with the Chinese leader and with his wife, Sun Ching-ling, who was lively and charming although she took the revolution as seriously as her husband. In the next three years Cohen served Dr. Sun in many ways, some dramatic, some dangerous and some foolish.

Dr. Sun stayed on in Shanghai month after month, spending most of his time writing again. In 1920 he had published a book about the international development of China, in English. Now he edited a Chinese periodical called the *Reconstruction Miscellany* in which he discussed reasons why the revolution had failed, and also published many other articles. He was always in demand for lectures. A favorite theme was still the question of a railroad system for China. *Memoirs of a Chinese Revolutionary* was begun during this time in Shanghai, and would appear first in Russian and then in an English version in 1927.

This time of writing, lecturing, and consulting in Shanghai stopped suddenly in 1923 because Dr. Sun was able to return to Canton. Funds to carry out a campaign against the troublesome Chen Chiung-ming had been raised, and in January 1923, armies from the provinces of Yunnan and Kwangsi joined in Canton. Chen fled to

Waichow on the East River and disbanded his forces. This
was the very moment for Dr. Sun quickly to assert his leadership once more. He reached Hong Kong on February 20
and gave a speech at Hong Kong University, of which his
alma mater, Queen's College, later became a part. A crowd
of students carried him from the automobile to the auditorium, cheering as they went in a most embarrassing way.
The young people crowding into the large hall were wildly
enthusiastic. A ballot taken by the *Weekly Review of the
Far East* at that time put him at the top of China's list of
most esteemed men. He reached Canton three days after the
big meeting and concentrated on pulling the government
together. He made sure that he was elected president and
also that he was generalissimo, and he appointed Chiang
Kai-shek his chief-of-staff. The Canton of which he was now
leader had gone a long way toward becoming the model
city he had dreamed of, in its appearance, at least. The
changes had come about because of the young men there
who, in spite of warlords and faltering government, were
determined to show that a Chinese city could modernize.
The old city wall had been torn down and the bricks sal-
vaged from it had been crushed and used to improve roads
and boulevards. The waterfront where business houses
stood had been beautified and equipped with up-to-date
facilities. Public utilities had replaced old-fashioned methods and parks and playgrounds were planned. Those who
had seen the old city were astonished at the change that had
been brought about.

In the summer of 1923 Dr. Sun sent Chiang to Moscow
to study Russian military methods, for he was convinced
that Russia understood good military practice as well as
revolution. Yet it was hard for him to turn away from

Western powers and commit himself to Russian methods, and he made one more appeal to his old friends. When the American Minister Jacob Gould Shurman visited Canton, Dr. Sun talked with him asking him to approach Great Britain, France and the other powers to see whether they would help China over a five-year period. Dr. Sun had worked out an astonishing plan under which the capitals of all the provinces would be controlled by foreign military occupation forces. His idea was that foreigners with experience in democratic procedures could put the provincial governments in order, hold elections, train administrators, and then leave.

It was a desperate proposal, but Dr. Sun was desperate. He was growing old and sometimes a spasm of pain gripped him in the side. Of course the American official would never support such a scheme as Dr. Sun's and it went no further. From now on the Chinese leader turned more and more against the Western powers who were in China and claimed that she was their victim. It was true that the Salt Commission and the Maritime Customs were in foreign hands and other injustices certainly existed. Dr. Sun at last declared himself ready to cooperate with any country that would help overthrow the Peking government but he told an American who interviewed him that the only country that showed any sign of helping the Kuomintang in the south was the Soviet government of Russia.

Russia did not wait for encouragement. A newspaper correspondent named Michael Borodin arrived in Canton in October. Even though he was really an agent of the Russian Communist Party, Dr. Sun turned to him quite openly for help. Everyone else seemed to have abandoned China, he thought. Whether he had justifiable reasons to feel this

way or not, was not the question. The important thing was
time. It was running out. In December 1923 Dr. Sun told a
great audience in the Canton YMCA, "We no longer look
to the Western powers. Our faces are turned toward Russia."[1]

Borodin knew how to work with Dr. Sun, and he was not
easy to work with. The Russian was careful not to destroy
his dreams or pooh-pooh his impractical plans, but managed to win the Chinese leader over. He knew that every
great movement needed a magnetic personality, one whose
ideals attracted followers. Dr. Sun had both magnetism and
ideals. He was just the one to lead a program that could
gradually be directed toward increasing the strength of
Communism in China. In less than a month after his arrival
in Canton, Borodin had mellowed Dr. Sun's feelings about
Communists who were working for that Party becoming
members of the Kuomintang. Dr. Sun welcomed an important Communist leader into it and no longer even suggested
that Communists who joined the Kuomintang ought to stop
working in the Communist Party. He declared that everyone had to unite their efforts for the sake of their country.

Chiang Kai-shek returned from his study in Moscow at the
end of 1923 with the promise of military advisers who
would help in organizing a new Chinese army and in estab-
lishing a proposed military academy. The new academy,
called Whampoa Military Academy, soon became famous
and many more students than could possibly be enrolled
applied. By June 1924 more than thirty Russian advisers
had arrived to help in the work with the army and to in-
struct in the new school. One was Galen, later famous as
General Blücher, who was put in command of the training

of the cadets. He also later helped to get arms from Russia for Dr. Sun.

Labor was organized under Michael Borodin's guidance, but the more important part he played was in helping Dr. Sun reorganize the Kuomintang itself. The future of China lay in its hands. Dr. Sun and the Russian spent many hours discussing how delegates ought to be chosen for the First National Congress, for not much machinery had yet been set up. The Russian met with Chinese leaders as well as with Dr. Sun; it was finally settled that Dr. Sun would choose some representatives himself, and local branches of the party that were still in existence would choose the rest. The sessions of the congress were then very carefully planned. At last the congress met for the first time, on January 20, 1924. Dr. Sun gave the opening speech. He expressed some ideas that were new to most of the Chinese leaders when he said, "All members of the party must possess spiritual unity. In order that all the members may be united spiritually, the first thing is to sacrifice freedom, the second is to offer ability. If the individual can sacrifice his freedom, then the whole party will have freedom. If the individual can offer his ability, then the whole party will possess ability."[2] He was asking for devotion to a cause and forgetfulness of self. Few liked what he said and some believed that Borodin's influence upon him showed.

The important outcome of this first meeting of the congress was the new constitution that was written after it closed. This constitution planned a one-party government, or rule by the Kuomintang or Nationalist Party.

Michael Borodin was sensitive to many aspects of the Kuomintang situation. He saw that Dr. Sun wanted credit for his devotion to China's revolution and for any progress that was made. Borodin also saw that Dr. Sun was very anxious that China should take a place among the world's great powers, but her revolution had failed so often that she had lost rather than gained status. Borodin tried to give Dr. Sun the feeling that China's revolution was part of a world rejection of imperialism. For that reason, he said, China should join Russia in a world brotherhood, the Third International, that was devoted to bringing a new day.

Dr. Sun's gift in speaking could help, too, in supporting Borodin's hopes and in building up a greater and greater following for the Kuomintang. The response of audiences everywhere could not but reassure the Chinese leader, as well as win friends. Borodin pushed him forward on lecture tours, while he himself stayed far in the background. As soon as the congress meeting was well over, Dr. Sun was in constant demand. Fifty-four of his speeches would later be published as *Collected Works*. His lectures were given before all kinds of groups. His manner was casual, even blunt, but his theme was usually some variation of his Three Principles, which he acknowledged he had first gotten from Abraham Lincoln. Speeches on this subject were collected and published as *San Min Chu I* or *Three Principles of the People*. He became famous and important to China's future largely because of them.

16. Expedition to the North: Death

China was divided into two parts, their capitals at Peking and Canton. While Dr. Sun was trying to make his ideas clear through his lectures, and while he was shoring up the Kuomintang government in the south by leaning on the help Russia offered, things were happening in Peking that would undermine the progress he was making.

In 1923 a warlord in the north named Tsao Kun managed to oust President Li Yuan-hung and get himself elected president by bribing people to vote for him. The affair was so scandalous that news of it spread across the country in an angry wave. Two factions now developed, that of Tsao Kun and his military leader, Wu Pei-fu, and that of Chang Tso-lin, who held great military power in Manchuria and who had many personal supporters. When fighting broke out between the factions in the north, Dr. Sun allied himself with Chang Tso-lin and, after he had issued a manifesto on the Northern Expedition, set out to join him. In his statement Dr. Sun declared that he was undertaking the expedition in order to destroy both traitors and imperialism.

A dramatic and a surprising event stopped Dr. Sun almost before he had started. One of the generals who was loyal to Chang Tso-lin, a man named Feng Yu-hsiang, known as the "Christian General" because he had joined a church, seized Peking in the name of the revolution by a *coup d' état.* He declared that he had taken the capital in the cause of democracy, and at once had the boy Emperor removed from his throne. Now, Feng announced, the North and the South must get together. He sent an invitation to Dr. Sun to come to Peking.

Dr. Sun could scarcely refuse to accept the invitation. His enemies had been defeated and he should meet those who were now his allies because of their victory, even though he knew that North and South were not ready to join. It was also important for him to go to Peking because the Karakhan Manifesto had been signed during this year and Karakhan was now the Russian ambassador to China, the first man of that rank ever sent to China by another country. He was naturally the leader of all the other foreign representatives. Michael Borodin urged Dr. Sun to go to Peking, too, and he also urged that he make speeches as he went. He knew that Dr. Sun would surely speak only well of Russia with things going as they were—the Karakhan Manifesto, the Whampoa Military Academy, and the help of the Russian advisers. Plans for the great trip were made. Before he left, the leaders in Canton gave Dr. Sun a dinner to celebrate his fifty-eighth birthday. It was a fine, heartwarming occasion and Dr. Sun did the unusual thing of sharing some of his personal memories with his guests.

On November 13, 1924, Dr. and Mrs. Sun and their staff

left Canton on a government cruiser for Hong Kong. From there they went by ocean liner to Shanghai stopping in Kobe, Japan, and then sailing on to Tientsin, the port for Peking. He could scarcely believe it when the International Settlement authorities in Shanghai at first refused to permit his landing because of his political activities. When he told the newspapermen who came aboard his ship that he was a Chinese and Shanghai was Chinese territory, they must have brought pressure on the authorities so that they relented. Perhaps they knew what the press could do if it championed a man or a cause. Dr. Sun was a worldwide figure now and anything he did made news for the watching eye of the public. So he went ashore, quietly triumphant, and to his own house at 29 Rue Molière. There he held a tea party for the friends who came to see him. Faithful Morris Cohen left him in Shanghai with a commission to secure arms in Canada. He never saw Dr. Sun again.

The little incident about landing in Shanghai is understandable because Dr. Sun was fearlessly speaking out against all foreigners and foreign imperialism whenever he had a chance. Even though he had barely managed to disembark, he made a speech of this kind in Shanghai. When he reached Kobe he declared that all of Asia ought to join to oppose European and American oppression. He spoke favorably of Russia, and most unfavorably of all of England, who as the leading colonial empire had "ruined" China. He made many speeches to large groups of students and they roared their approval of what he said.

From Kobe Dr. Sun went on to Tientsin by a Japanese ship. The sea was rough. The winds were cold and strong. He was unable to eat anything, not because of seasickness but because of the pain that gripped him more and more often. When he reached Tientsin on the night of December 4, the shore and landing were teeming with cheering crowds. Even though he was shivering and those who were nearest him saw that he did not really hear questions that were addressed to him, he began to speak for the principles he believed in in a voice that was strong and clear. He declared that he had come to reorganize the country, North and South, on a basis that would include all progressive groups, and give the people the right to say how they wanted to be governed. He acted as though he were still in Canton rather than in Tientsin, enemy country. The arc lights that blazed down made his face look ashen. The wind that whipped from across the northern plains was biting. He did not even try to smile, but he would not give in to pain or cold. Now he was face to face with Peking in a confrontation he had planned and wanted for many years, and he was all the more determined to make a strong stand because of rumors he had heard. These rumors indicated that his recommendations for unification had already been rejected, that the invitation he was accepting under such painful circumstances was not what it had appeared to be.

The afternoon of the next day he went to make an official call on Chang Tso-lin, with whom he had allied himself. They talked for three hours. When he returned to his hotel where his headquarters were set up, he was so cold and ill that he had to go to bed. The doctors who examined him said that he had influenza as well as some trouble with his liver. He stayed in bed unwillingly until the influenza was cured but he would not pay any attention to the pains. Callers came and went in a steady stream.

Among those who came were representatives from the Peking government who presented their plans. Dr. Sun saw that, as the rumors had said, all his recommendations had been rejected. It was hard for him to believe it. He must go on to Peking himself amd face this daring action. Peking was only a matter of a comparatively few miles on, he told his staff and family. Yet he waited a little longer, resting in bed to gather more strength. While he waited, even worse news reached him. President Tsao Kun had already sent official notes to the foreign legations saying that China would observe the rules of extraterritoriality, or their old treaty rights, one of the main things he had openly declared against. Dr. Sun flew into a rare fury and refused to stay in bed any longer, asking wildly why he had been invited north at all. When he was at last gotten back to bed, he had a raging fever.

Nothing would make him change his mind about going on to Peking. Ten days after his fever dropped, he started out in a special coach, accompanied by his party, for the Hotel de Pekin. When he reached there on the last day of the year (1924) he was too weary to smile and almost too weak to speak. But his mind was still concentrating on the dream of joining North and South, the details of which were to be worked out at a reorganization conference he had been planning. Russian and German doctors attended him and he tried to rally his strength for what lay ahead. Outside the hotel, crowds waited, and the word "cancer" was whispered from one to another, although some did not even know what it meant.

Still people came to see him. From one of them Dr. Sun discovered that the chairman of the reorganization conference and the cabinet that had been selected were almost all followers of the old monarchy. He clearly had been betrayed. This journey north had been a cruel farce. He an-

grily forbade any members of the Kuomintang to take part
in the reorganization conference.

Now his illness grew quickly worse and on January 24,
he was moved to Peking Union Medical College Hospital,
which was at that time the most modern medical institution
in China. An American doctor operated on him in the hope
of removing the cancer, but it had gone too far for that, so
X-ray treatment was tried. Since there was no hope of his
recovering, Wellington Koo, a personal friend, came and
moved him to his own home. Mrs. Sun, Sun Fo, and a grand-
son were with him all the time now. Friends often came to
see him but he was too weak to do more than grasp their
hands. Worse than his illness was the fact that he knew his
enemies, China's enemies, had defeated him. His whole life's
purpose seemed to have failed. Although even those who
opposed his ideas were courteous toward an elder in the
time-honored manner of his country, he knew that they
were steadily opposing all he stood for. He did not let his
despair show on his masklike face, but those who were close
beside his bed at night knew that he was weeping.

By the end of February it was common knowledge that
Dr. Sun would not live much longer. He had no will prepared, no final statement drawn up for his country. One
afternoon when he seemed to be sinking, some of the family
who were important leaders, and Wang Ching-wei, who had
been his friend since those days in 1904 when Dr. Sun had
stayed with a Chinese pastor in New York, suggested drafting a statement and then reading it to him. He could then
sign it if it pleased him. When Dr. Sun did not respond to
their suggestion, Wang Ching-wei wrote a tentative statement and read it to him. Dr. Sun listened carefully but did
not say anything for a long time. Then suddenly he said

quite clearly, "I have really nothing to say now. If I recover I shall go to a resort in the Western Hills near Peking and recuperate and then I shall have plenty of time to talk with you. But if I am going to die, it is useless to say anything."[1] His mind was not on a will but on Canton, where General Chiang Kai-shek, at the head of the revolutionary armies, was attacking the forces of Chen Chiung-ming, who had caused so much trouble. Recent reports were encouraging, and Dr. Sun ordered a telegram sent to Chiang in Canton asking him not to let the citizens of the city suffer.

Late on the afternoon of March 11, Dr. Sun requested someone to bring him the will documents, the one prepared for the public and another which the family had asked for, and while his wife held his hand, he signed them. Now a waiting silence filled the room. At last Dr. Sun spoke. He said that he had come north in hopes of convoking a people's convention and implementing his Three Principles. He said it did not matter to him personally whether he lived or died, but that it broke his heart to see the failure of the purposes to which he had devoted his life. He paused and again a silence fell over the waiting and watching family. Then he called for his brother-in-law and said, "You are a Christian; I too am a Christian. . . . I am a messenger of God to help men to obtain equality and freedom."[2]

The next morning, March 12, 1925, Dr. Sun Yat-sen died.

Russia responded to the news at once by sending a telegram from Stalin in the name of the Russian Communist Party and then a second one from the Third International, her worldwide organization. Russia also advised the Chinese leaders to have Dr. Sun's body embalmed for indefinite public viewing, a thing never done in China. Peking Union

Medical College undertook to do it. Mrs. Sun requested
that a Christian memorial service be held in the college's
beautiful auditorium. Remembering how Dr. Sun had loved
the robed choir of the Anglican school which he had attended in Honolulu as a boy, a procession with a surpliced
choir carrying candles followed his coffin and sang his
favorite hymns at the memorial service. Dr. Sun had not
been a church attender for many years. One day he had
said, "I do not belong to the Christianity of the churches,
but to the Christianity of Jesus who was a revolutionary."[3]
Now his family saw that a large proportion of those at
his memorial service were Westerners and missionaries.

The coffin was taken to an imperial pavilion in Central
Park, part of what was once enclosed in the Imperial City,
escorted by students who fought for places near the bier,
their banners waving in the chill spring air. Karakhan, the
Soviet ambassador, was the chief mourner. The body lay in
state draped with the Kuomintang flag, a red flag with a
twelve-rayed white sun on a blue field.

For three weeks crowds, including school children who
were given a special holiday, came to gaze at the waxen
face beneath the glass-covered casket while a phonograph
played recordings of Dr. Sun's speeches. Probably few listened to the words. Most seemed to be numbed by the sud-
den realization that this man who now lay dead had
brought China to a new day; that unlike the leaders they
had known before, he had not grown rich in holding a high
position in his country; he had not tried to make himself
safe and secure; he had not resorted to bribery to win supporters and friends. He was a new kind of Chinese leader,
and although he was dead, his real influence was just beginning to come to life.

Dr. Sun himself could never have guessed how much greater he would become after he had died than he had been while he was alive. A wave of patriotic nationalism began to sweep across the country. Students in Shanghai, protesting imperialism with its unequal treaties and foreign concessions, were shot down by police fire only two months after his death. In Hong Kong a long boycott against British goods and authority brought more shooting. In September Moscow opened the Sun Yat-sen University with the aim of teaching Chinese students Soviet culture and methods of revolution. When the Second National Congress met in Canton in January 1926, Dr. Sun's will was read and declared a sacred document. All his other writings, too, were accepted as basic documents of the Kuomintang and no one spoke against them. Weekly memorial services were made compulsory for all the branches of the Kuomintang, in government offices and committee meetings, in factories, barracks and all schools. During this service everyone bowed three times to a portrait of Dr. Sun, listened to the reading of his will, and then held three minutes of meditation. Sometimes a short patriotic address followed the silence, and then everyone sang the Kuomintang national anthem, which was based on the Three Principles.

Dr. Sun's influence spread across China, but it especially touched a young general who had come to know him well during hot weeks spent together on a small gunboat on the Pearl River near Canton. He would be the one finally to complete the long-dreamed-of Northern Expedition in the name of the revolution. The only trouble was that although he had become well acquainted with the now sainted leader, he had never really understood why he should be so devoted to the idea of freedom and equality for everyone, without any thought for himself. What Dr. Sun had begun was left for Chiang Kai-shek to complete. But no military leader could make Dr. Sun's dream come true, for he had dreamed of a new China based on principles rather than mere power.

BIBLIOGRAPHY

Abend, Hallett, *My Life in China*. New York, Harcourt Brace, 1943.

Chen, Stephen, and Robert Payne, *Sun Yat-sen, a Portrait*. New York, The John Day Company, 1946.

Clubb, O. Edmund, *Twentieth Century China*. New York and London, Columbia University Press, 1964.

Drage, Charles, *Two-Gun Cohen*. New York and London, Harper and Bros., 1948.

Fairbank, John King, *The United States and China*. Cambridge, Massachusetts, Harvard University Press, 1958.

Fitzgerald, C. P., *The Birth of Communist China*. Baltimore, Penguin Books, 1964.

Hahn, Emily, *Chiang Kai-shek*. New York, Doubleday and Company, 1955.

———, *China Only Yesterday: 1850–1950*. New York, Doubleday and Company, 1963.

Isaacs, Harold R., *The Tragedy of the Chinese Revolution*. Stanford, California, Stanford University Press, 1961.

Leng, Shao Chuan, and Palmer, Norman, *Sun Yat-sen and Communism*. New York, Frederick A. Praeger, and The Foreign Policy Research Institute of the University of Pennsylvania, 1960.

Linebarger, Paul, *Sun Yat-sen and the Chinese Republic.* New York and London, The Century Company, 1925.

Sharman, Lyon, *Sun Yat-sen, His Life and Its Meaning.* New York, The John Day Company, 1934.

Selle, Earle A., *Donald of China.* New York and London, Harper and Bros., 1948.

Sun Yat-sen, *The Three Principles of the People (San Min Chu I),* trans. by Frank W. Price. Shanghai, China, The China Committee, Institute of Pacific Relations, 1927.

Tang, Liang-li, *The Inner History of the Chinese Revolution.* New York and London, The Century Company, 1925.

REFERENCES

CHAPTER 2
[1] *Sun Yat-sen and the Chinese Republic.* Paul Linebarger.
The Century Company, New York and London, 1925, p. 116.

CHAPTER 3
[1] *Sun Yat-sen and the Chinese Republic.* Paul Linebarger.
The Century Company, New York and London, 1925, p. 139.
[2] *Ibid.,* p. 140.
[3] *Sun Yat-sen, a Portrait.* Stephen Chen and Robert Payne.
The John Day Company, New York, 1946, p. 19.

CHAPTER 4
[1] From *The Missionary Herald,* Boston, April, 1912, p.
171 ff. as quoted in *Sun Yat-sen, His Life and Its Meaning.*
Lyon Sharman. The John Day Company, New York, 1934, p.
21.
[2] *Sun Yat-sen, a Portrait.* Stephen Chen and Robert Payne.
The John Day Company, New York, 1946, p. 25.

CHAPTER 5
[1] *Sun Yat-sen, His Life and Its Meaning.* Lyon Sharman. The
John Day Company, New York, 1934, p. 46.
[2] *Ibid.,* p. 48.
[3] *Ibid.,* pp. 48, 49.

Chapter 7
    [1] *The True Solution of the Chinese Question*, Sun Yat-sen, 1904, as quoted in *Sun Yat-sen, His Life and Its Meaning.* Lyon Sharman. The John Day Company, New York, 1934, p. 89.

Chapter 8
    [1] The Inner History of the Chinese Revolution, T'ang Leang-li, as quoted in *Sun Yat-sen, His Life and Its Meaning.* Lyon Sharman. The John Day Company, New York, 1934, p. 98.

Chapter 10
    [1] *Sun Yat-sen, a Portrait.* Stephen Chen and Robert Payne. The John Day Company, New York, 1946, p. 99.
    [2] *Sun Yat-sen, His Life and Its Meaning.* Lyon Sharman. The John Day Company, New York, 1934, pp. 133, 134.
    [3] *Ibid.*, p. 137.

Chapter 12
    [1] *Sun Yat-sen, a Portrait.* Stephen Chen and Robert Payne. The John Day Company, New York, 1946, p. 143.
    [2] *Memoirs of a Chinese Revolutionary.* Sun Yat-sen. Hutchinson and Company, London, 1927, pp. 151–152.

Chapter 14
    [1] *Sun Yat-sen, a Portrait.* Stephen Chen and Robert Payne. The John Day Company, New York, 1946, p. 167.

Chapter 15
    [1] *Sun Yat-sen, His Life and Its Meaning.* Lyon Sharman. The John Day Company, New York, 1934, p. 253.
    [2] *Ibid.*, p. 257.

Chapter 16
    [1] *Sun Yat-sen, a Portrait.* Stephen Chen and Robert Payne. The John Day Company, New York, 1946, pp. 216, 217.
    [2] *Ibid.*, p. 220.
    [3] *Sun Yat-sen, His Life and Its Meaning.* Lyon Sharman. The John Day Company, New York, 1934, p. 310.

CHRONOLOGY

1866 Sun Yat-sen born November 12, in Choyhung, Kwangtung Province.
1871 His eldest brother, Sun Mei, sailed for Honolulu.
1877 Sun Mei returned to Choyhung on business.
1879 Sun Yat-sen sailed for Honolulu and entered Iolani School.
1882 Sun Yat-sen graduated from Iolani School.
1883 Returned to Choyhung, rebelled against superstitions, banished to Hong Kong for temple incident.
1884 Admitted to Queen's College in April; returned to Choyhung for marriage in May; sailed for Hawaii at Sun Mei's request in October.
1886 Returned to Canton in July; entered Pok Tsai Medical School, Canton, for one year.
1887 Transferred to Alice Memorial Hospital, Hong Kong.
1891 His son, Sun Fo, born October 18.
1892 Sun Yat-sen graduated from Alice Memorial Hospital Medical School; opened his own hospital in Macao.
1893 Moved hospital to Canton. Revolutionary activities develop.

1893   Sun Yat-sen and Lu Hao-tung went to Peking to interview Viceroy Li Hung-chang.

1894   Sun Yat-sen returned to Canton, sailed for Hawaii and founded Revive China Society there. Returned to Hong Kong in December.

1895   First attempt at revolution in Canton, September 9. After its failure, went to Hong Kong for safety; from there sailed for Honolulu by way of Japan, on first world tour.

1896   After six months in Honolulu sailed for San Francisco; from New York to London, arriving in Liverpool September 30; detained in Chinese legation October 11 to 23.

1897.   Toured Europe rethinking meaning of revolution.

1898   Left London for Japan; in Yokahama when Boxer uprising occurred in China in 1900.

1900   Second attempt at revolution took place in August, at Waichow, Kwangtung.

1903   Began second world tour after visits to Annam (Vietnam).

1905   Established Tung Meng Hui in Japan in September.

1906   Uprising took place in Hunan Province in October.

1907   Third and fourth revolutionary attempts made during April; failed. Sun Yat-sen banished from French-held territory, escaped to Singapore.

1908   Huang Hsing made four more revolutionary attempts from Annam border. All failed and he had to withdraw. Eight revolutionary attempts had been made.
Empress Dowager Tzu Hsi died just after Emperor Kuang Hsu. Child Emperor Pu Yi enthroned.

1909   Sun Yat-sen set out on third (and last) world tour.

1910   Ninth attempted revolution failed in Canton; Sun Yat-sen broke his tour and returned to Penang, Malaya; then resumed tour.

1911   Tenth revolutionary attempt failed in Canton in March; the real revolution broke out in Wuchang on October 10. Sun Yat-sen arrived in Shanghai December 24. Representatives of the provinces declared their independence of Peking, met in Nanking and elected Sun Yat-sen provisional president of republic of China.

1912 Sun Yat-sen resigned February 14; national assembly elected Yuan Shih-kai provisional president; he took office March 10, Sun Yat-sen arrived in Peking in August. Kuomintang replaced Tung Meng Hui, August 25. Sun Yat-sen opened Bureau of Railway Development in Shanghai in October.

1913 Sun Yat-sen sailed for Japan in February, returned March 25. Sung Chiao-jen assassinated in Shanghai March 10. April 27 Yuan Shih-kai opened negotiations for Five-Power Reorganization Loan.

July 12: Second Revolution began.

July 20: Chiang Kai-shek and Chen Chi-mei attacked Shanghai.

July 23: Sun Yat-sen removed from position of Director of Railway Development.

October 10: Yuan Shih-kai assumed full presidency; November 3 he dissolved Kuomintang. Republic of China recognized by foreign powers.

1914 Parliament instituted by national assembly, suspended by Yuan Shih-kai. In Japan Sun Yat-sen inaugurated new Chinese Revolutionary Party. October 25 he married Soong Ching-ling.

1915 Japanese Minister in Peking presented Twenty-One Demands to Yuan Shih-kai; accepted May 9.

Third Revolution attempted in Yunnan Province.

1916 Yuan Shih-kai became emperor January 1; restored republic March 22; died June 6. Li Yuan-hung became president.

Sun Yat-sen returned to China in June.

Parliament reconvened in August.

1917 August 14: China declared war against Austria and Germany.

Sun Yat-sen called parliament to meet in Canton; military government set up there; Sun Yat-sen elected generalissimo.

1918   May 4: Sun Yat-sen resigned and left for Shanghai.

1919   Student Movement protesting terms of Shantung settle-
       ment at Paris Foreign Ministers' Conference, preliminary
       to Versailles Peace Treaty, began and swept country.

1920   Sun Yat-sen sent orders to Canton to end rival factions;
       the Chinese Revolutionary Party merged with the Kuo-
       mintang.

1921   Parliament of southern government met in Canton,
       elected Sun Yat-sen president, inaugurating him May 5.

1922   Sun Yat-sen headed Northern Expedition to Peking in
       October; returned because factions developed there; re-
       sumed expedition in spring, returning to Canton June 1.

1922   Revolt in Canton, June 16; Sun Yat-sen's life threatened;
       escaped to cruiser *Yung Feng*, then to Hong Kong and
       Shanghai. Made worldwide proclamation from Shanghai
       August 15.

1923   Sun Yat-sen interviewed Russian Adolf Joffe in Shanghai.
       Returned to Canton in February; sent Chiang Kai-shek
       to Moscow to study in summer 1923.

1924   January 20: First National Congress convened according
       to Kuomintang constitution, in Canton.
       June 16: Whampoa Military Academy opened in Canton.
       October 18: Sun Yat-sen started on Northern Expedition
       again.
       Feng Yu-hsiang seized Peking in name of the revolution,
       for Chang Tso-lin, whom Sun Yat-sen backed; Sun Yat-
       sen delayed expedition; invited to capital for talks about
       reorganization; started December 31.

1925   Sun Yat-sen suspected betrayal; fell seriously ill; sus-
       picions verified.
       Documents of will drafted for him to sign; died March
       12.

Index

Index

About the Author

CORNELIA SPENCER was born in China and has written many books about the Orient, including *Ancient China, Made in China, Made in India, Made in Japan, Land of the Chinese People,* and *Understanding the Japanese People.* She has also written biographies of Jawaharlal Nehru, Harry S. Truman, Carlos P. Romulo, and the Soong sisters, as well as a series of histories of the great revolutions of mankind.